Echoing the Story

Echoing the Story

Living the Art of Listening

BRADY BRYCE

RESOURCE *Publications* · Eugene, Oregon

ECHOING THE STORY
Living the Art of Listening

Copyright © 2010 Brady Bryce. All rights reserved. Except for brief quotations in critical publications or reviews, no part of this book may be reproduced in any manner without prior written permission from the publisher. Write: Permissions, Wipf and Stock Publishers, 199 W. 8th Ave., Suite 3, Eugene, OR 97401.

Resource Publications
An Imprint of Wipf and Stock Publishers
199 W. 8th Ave., Suite 3
Eugene, OR 97401
www.wipfandstock.com

ISBN 13: 978-1-60899-818-0

Manufactured in the U.S.A.

All scripture quotations, unless otherwise indicated, are taken from the New Revised Standard Version Bible, copyright 1989, Division of Christian Education of the National Council of the Churches of Christ in the United States of America. Used by permission. All rights reserved.

To the One whose echo invigorates the human soul

Contents

Preface ix
Acknowledgments xi
Introduction xiii

Week One 1
    Read—Narrating Life Together
    Discuss—Small Group Conversation
    Practice—Echoes of God Activity

Week Two 13
    Read—God Creates a Covenant People
    Discuss—Small Group Conversation
    Practice—Echoes of God Activity
    Reflect—The Story & My Story

Week Three 23
    Read—God Rules and Pursues His People
    Discuss—Small Group Conversation
    Practice—Echoes of God Activity
    Reflect—The Story & My Story

Week Four 32
    Read—God Judges Unfaithfulness to Covenant
    Discuss—Small Group Conversation
    Practice—Echoes of God Activity
    Reflect—The Story & My Story

Week Five 41
    Read—God Remains Faithful
    Discuss—Small Group Conversation
    Practice—Echoes of God Activity
    Reflect—The Story & My Story

WEEK SIX 50
    Read—God's People Respond in Worship and Wisdom
    Discuss—Small Group Conversation
    Practice—Echoes of God Activity
    Reflect—The Story & My Story

WEEK SEVEN 59
    Read—God Lives Among His People
    Discuss—Small Group Conversation
    Practice—Echoes of God Activity
    Reflect—The Story & My Story

WEEK EIGHT 68
    Read—God Enters Into His People
    Discuss—Small Group Conversation
    Practice—Echoes of God Activity
    Reflect—The Story & My Story

WEEK NINE 78
    Read—God Preaches the Gospel to Everyone
    Discuss—Small Group Conversation
    Practice—Echoes of God Activity
    Reflect—The Story & My Story

WEEK TEN 88
    Read—God's Covenant is Life in Christ
    Discuss—Small Group Conversation
    Practice—Echoes of God Activity
    Reflect—The Story & My Story

WEEK ELEVEN 97
    Read—God Makes Everything New
    Discuss—Small Group Conversation
    Practice—Echoes of God Activity
    Reflect—The Story & My Story

WEEK TWELVE 107
    Read—The Whole Story of God in One Story
    Reflect—The Story & My Story Journaling Exercise
    Discuss—Small Group Assessment Exercise Conversation
    Practice—Identify Next Listening Adventure

Bibliography 117

Preface

Using the Guidebook with a Group

What is this guidebook *about?* A small group of people will experience the whole Bible as "The Story of God." Plus, this group will become more aware of God's story continued in everyday life. Participants will practice listening to the stories of others and to life (see Introduction).

Why should I participate? If you have ever wondered how the Bible fits together, then you should read this guidebook. If you have ever wondered how the story of God connects with human stories, then you should participate. If you are interested in a small group experience that combines healthy teaching and reading with lively community sharing and spiritual reflection, then this experience is for you. Learn how to pay attention to God's echoes in people's stories.

Will there be homework? Yes, outside the group gatherings you will read a chapter on the story of God prior to a group meeting (15-30 minutes). Plus, as a follow-up to the group you may participate in a listening activity called "Echoes of God," where you listen and observe life for indications of God. Finally, you are provided with some Bible readings and reflection questions to use in your quiet time, coffee break, or lunch time (15-30 minutes) for five days each week.

How much time am I committing? The group meets for twelve weeks. The weekly small group is 60 minutes. Your reading and reflection will average about 20 minutes the other days of the week. This may seem like a lot, but this disciplined community experience is a spiritually rich daily discipline. Remember, the Bible covers thousands of years and you will experience an overview of the whole Bible in only three months.

Who can benefit from this process? This guidebook is intended for people who want to experience the story of God and see God working in the lives of outsiders to faith. This small group of people will experience how our human stories can be viewed in light of the story of God. Adaptations of this program have been used with a wide range of participants: middle school kids, college students, adults, Sunday morning sermon crowd, and even with low-income, uneducated non-believers. While this program provides you with a great deal of content, the focus is discovering the story of God in everyday human stories.

Who should lead? Most dedicated Christians can lead this study. This program is demanding initially on leaders, who must learn to listen and reflect, rather than trying to teach this as a class. However, the guidebook prepares you to lead by listening to others—not by speaking or answering. The best preparation for leading a group through this experience is to read through the guidebook with another person. Many find that once they go through this experience once they want to lead the same material over and over again. Each time one comes to God's story it is a brand new experience.

Acknowledgments

I AM NOT MY own but am dependent upon others. Any good in this work is an echo of God. Every error or inaccuracy is my own. The love and prayers of others made this conversation a joy. The Singing Oaks Church of Christ in Denton, Texas—my spiritual family and co-workers in ministry—allowed me space to explore the story with others. My students at Abilene Christian University inspire and bless me as together we explore narrative evangelism. Thanks to the many readers and conversation partners on this project: Dr. Richard Peace, Jackie King, Tom and Linda Blucker, José Fetzer, Justin and Lizzie Ross, Dr. Leroy Garrett, and Ouida Garrett. Thanks to my friends at the Rosemont Apartments who still gather and talk about God's activity in their lives. Thanks to my editors Christian Amondson and Jim Tedrick along with others like Lisa Marie Sandoval and Kate Miller who reduced my mistakes. My dear sister, Kelly Taylor, read many editions to provide countless corrections. My parents Dean and Jeanine are my ministers, who read, edited, and encouraged me through a lifetime of education. My children Nathan and Lizzie are my most valuable professors. I love my exquisite wife Donna who surrounds me with love, prayers, and assistance. Donna is my partner in a lifetime of listening to God. To each one who enters the words of this story: together may we learn the art of echoing God's life with our lips and lives.

Introduction

THE STORY BEGINS

A STORY EMBRACES EVERYONE. The first lines of an opening scene can transport us inside the world of a story. Before we enter the story, you deserve to know why the process explored in this guidebook is worth your admission ticket. Why should one listen to these stories or bother to learn the spiritual practice of echoing the story of God?

First, I believe that God is already at work in the lives of every person. Regardless of your belief about or recognition of God—God is already working in your life. Without my words or my help, God works in this world. It makes no difference whether one is a believer or a doubter, atheist or activist, theologian or gardener. God is present in every person's story.

Most followers of Jesus do not really believe God is at work. We act as if God cannot show up until we speak, start a church, or put people into a program. The premise of this process is that God tells his story on the pages of human life. You could choose not to participate in this story, but this is your invitation to enter the theatre of this story with some other people over a few weeks. Believers, doubters, skeptics, and agnostics may watch a grand story unfold on the everyday pages of human hearts and throughout the history of faith as expressed in the Bible.

Second, the world would be a better place if more Christians would shut-up. Most talk way too much. Christians have too many answers and words and not enough positive action in our world. Our first action is to close our mouths and listen. The world does not want or need more words, but most people welcome our active listening. Followers of Jesus need training to learn how to listen and enter a conversation with their ears first.

A listening approach actually imitates God, who is more inclined to silence than speech. Because I trust that God is already at work, my mission is to strain my ears listening for God's work echoing in the lives of others. When I hear the echoes of God's activity, then I will speak up and point them out.

Third, people can learn how to hear the echoes of God's activity. While it may be difficult to close our mouths and believe God is speaking without us, the spiritual practice of listening is a learnable skill. Learning to swim takes practice, repetition, and training. Becoming a listener who is slow to speak is like a swim student learning to trust their body will float on its own without flailing violently at the water. These pages will float you through a simple process that requires attentive practice. Before this introduction ends, I will share a simple group process for learning how to listen for God in the stories of others. During this several week process you will not only begin to hear echoes of God's activity in life, but you also will be equipped to listen to others.

Several years ago I came across an ancient verse that reflects my guiding thought. The quote is credited to a Middle Eastern man. He felt trapped in the darkness of life yet walked through darkness by trusting the name of God. The prophet Isaiah writes, "The Lord God has given me the tongue of a teacher, that I may know how to sustain the weary with a word. Morning by morning he wakens—wakens my ear to listen as those who are taught" (50:4).

Just as I believe that God is already at work in your life (for the most part in unrecognized ways) I also believe that teaching is primarily a gift of listening. A teacher listens to learn students' perspectives and knowledge in order to be the best guide. Many of the best teachers are listeners and observers. My prayer is that every day God will "wake up my ears to listen as those who learn" so that he can use me to provide words to weary travelers. So, I rehearse quietness in the presence of others and then speak up when God makes himself known through a story or phrase, a joke or a throw away comment.

This listening gift is not unique to me. I think that you have it too. If you are interested then I will help you practice this gift. This thin guidebook is a journey in listening that will help you enter the world with your ears first. By listening to the words on these pages, listening to new friends in a small group, hearing the words of scripture, and tuning your soul to practice hearing the echoes of God, you can uncover this gift.

My desire is for people to come to know God. Not merely to know *about* God or know of God but also to know God *as a friend* acting with them in love. I believe this happens through experiencing life with other people. More specifically, we can discover God through the living stories of Scripture and by leafing through the moments of our day. This process is an exercise routine for developing attentiveness to God in the narratives of Scripture, other people, and ourselves. Then the Bible will no longer be a book carried around but a conversation partner as we listen for the voice of God every day.

REDEFINING CATECHESIS AS ECHOING

This guidebook seeks God through stories. Christians need to listen for the contemporary activity of God in the lives of people, whether they are listening to believers, non-believers, or anti-believers in Jesus Christ. One of the ancient words for teaching or instruction is "catechesis." The verb form of catechesis also means "to resound from above" or "to echo."

Today the common images associated with a formal catechesis program are the classroom; lecture hall; or, lines of desks, tests, homework, and teachers. In a modern classroom there is a clear distinction between teachers and students. A podium separates seated students from the standing expert. A teacher speaks and students take notes. Catechesis, in a modern context, is specialized instruction provided by churches to teach the Christian faith that involves students and teachers, information and memorization, lessons and lectures.

The word "catechesis" did not originate with the church or religion. It appeared in the Greek world of poetry, drama, and acting. In a dramatic context, this word pictures an actor echoing the lines of a play from a stage to an audience below. The theatre seat is different from the classroom desk. Rather than describing an actor on the stage echoing his lines to the theatre audience, the early church pushed the passive meaning to "be informed" or "receive news." Therefore, learning meant echoing the correct answers to doctrinal questions. The teacher asks a question and the student echoes the correct fact, doctrine, or tradition.

My theatre definition for catechesis captures this earlier pre-Christian word usage that pictures a poet echoing lines to a live audience. This image is potent for new catechesis practice, because in this guidebook actors replace teachers and the desk is one of many props on the stage. So forget the desk image and think about a stage, a place where story acts and moves. The stage of life locates our story as part of the story of God.

While there is nothing wrong with learning and repeating core truths, there is another way to experience catechesis as echoing. The simplest way to summarize the purpose of this guidebook is in one sentence: This guidebook aims *to take a small group of people through a process of listening for God and echoing the activity of God in life.* This experience prepares people to listen for echoes of God within the lives of others.

Picture again the theatre. You, a believer, are like an offstage director calling out the forgotten lines, pointing to the deeper elements of the story, reminding the actors of the larger story, and enjoying the performance of life. The people of the world are like actors on the stage. We live our lives oblivious to the story of God's working in the world. Actually many people do not believe in God and may reject the notion of God. However, these actors unknowingly play their lives to the audience of God. God is the one who applauds.

God is beyond time. God is at work in all things. Whether or not a person believes in God, God still acts. Our task as learners is to become aware of God's activity and begin to participate with God in the story rather than ignore God. When we perceive God's story in people's lives then we point it out.

ECHOING IN THE STORY

Let's explore catechesis as echoing God's activity from the Bible. Jesus grew up in the Jewish tradition with its rich history of instructive family practices and traditions. Festivals like the Passover were experiences of retelling the Exodus story of how Yahweh God delivered the Hebrew people from slavery. Families retold the stories of God's activity among them. Even the practice of rabbis instructing disciples seems like catechesis. Disciples follow rabbis, listen to their teaching, and observe their lives.

The word "catechesis" is never used in the Old Testament and it is rare in the New Testament. The rarity of catechesis in the New Testament especially is surprising, because its documents were written to teach the way of Jesus. Regardless, the seven uses of catechesis do reveal a uniquely Christian concept that is worth a brief exploration.

The most obvious instance occurs twice in Galatians 6:6 "Those who are *taught* (echoed) the word must share in all good things with their *teacher* (echoer)." "Teach" is the right translation of catechesis, but imagine the story behind the word. Those who hear echoes must share what they hear with the one echoing.

This verse alters the typical classroom separation between teacher and students as speaker and listeners, expert and trainees. This verse surprises us in how the top down teaching relationship is, in a subtle way, reversed as the teacher listens to students. Both student and teacher hear echoes from above and sound off what they hear to others.

The apostle Paul selects this echoing word—catechesis, not found in Hebrew Scriptures—to describe teaching the law. He labels pre-Christian Jews as those *"instructed* (echoed) in the law" (Romans 2:18). In fact, Paul prefers speaking a few clear words of *instruction* (echoing) than millions of words in another language (1 Corinthians 14:19). But this is not about listening to teaching but action on teaching. God justifies those who live the law and not just hear the law (Romans 2:13). So, Paul, like Jesus, believes listening is necessary, but it demands action (see also Matthew 7:21, 24–27).

Another important New Testament story using the word "catechesis" is with Apollos. In this passage two Greek verbs, "to echo" and "to teach," are tied together in the same context. Apollos "had been *instructed* (echoed) in the Way of the Lord; and he spoke with burning enthusiasm and *taught* (teaches) accurately the things concerning Jesus" (Acts 18:25). Faith instruction naturally leads to faith sharing. This same association is loosely present in the second chapter of Romans. Those instructed in the law (2:18) are encouraged to teach others (2:21). In other words, to be taught properly will result in becoming an "echoer" of that new learning. Certainly, people who are instructed must take the next step of communicating in word and action what they have learned. "Catechesis" is a unique word for passing on (or echoing) the Christian faith.

A final New Testament example is taken from the introduction of Luke's gospel. Doctor Luke writes a two-part document (Luke—Acts) to *instruct* (echo) Theophilus (Luke 1:1–4). We do not know whether Theophilus is a non-Christian learning about Jesus for the first time or a Christian learning more about Jesus. This distinction is insignificant. In either situation, it is still true that passing down faith took place through this written document about the life, ministry, passion, and resurrection of Jesus.

In closing, there are three lessons to hear from how catechesis is used in the New Testament. First, Christian catechesis pictures listeners hearing something echoed or taught from above. Second, the student and the teacher share the roles of listening and echoing the faith. Third, the Christian faith's primary content is echoing the person and work of Jesus. Catechesis is an adventure of becoming one with God's story by echoing the reality of God in the commonness of life.

HOW TO USE THIS GUIDEBOOK

This book is a guided experience in the story of God. Rarely can one explore the entirety of God's story in a short stretch of 12 weeks. While it contains loads of information, this guidebook is *not* about you downloading Bible content. So do not feel burdened to absorb the thousands of years of history and literature from each week's *Read* section. Instead, the group *Discuss* experience will raise your awareness of God's activity in Scripture and in everyday life. Cultivated with adults, middle school children, college students, and neighbors, this group approach is fertile enough to grow into a sermon series, an adult education ministry, small group discussion, or house church training. Different people acquired different things from this process. Long time Christians were amazed at the breadth of the story of God. Students grasped Scripture's theological framework. Others began to experience themselves right in the middle of God's story. So, while you may discover a lot of content and resources, remember that this process is about prayerfully addressing our lives to God and becoming aware of our part in the story of God.

There are four parts to the narrating process represented weekly: read, discuss, practice, and reflect. Each week you will read a short chapter that summarizes the story of God from the Bible (Read). Then, you will participate in a small group experience of prayer and conversation about life (Discuss), which is my favorite part. After the group, you have a question to experiment with listening for God's echoes in everyday life (Practice). Finally, you may choose to read passages from the Bible and reflect on how the story of God is being written in your life (Reflect). Week One gives an expanded description of this process.

The small group gathering (Discuss) is an amazing time of narrating life. While it will be more fully described in chapter 1 (p. 6) and experienced each week, a few introductory words are appropriate. *Discuss* contains four "moves" that allow participants time to listen and to share stories from their life. Amazingly these seemingly random experiences from our lives take on a collective meaning that echoes the activity of God. Our stories provide a setting for connections with each other. You will be surprised at how weekly reflecting on our lives through the same four questions in the opening sharing (for what are you thankful, how have you seen God at work, for what are you sorry, and who needs help) will stimulate your ears to hear the echoes of God. All four moves in the hour long small group (sharing, listening, telling, and connecting) narrate a group experience of a sacred reading of life, similar to the ancient practice of *lectio divina*.

Words are inadequate to describe the group experience of listening to stories for the echoes of God and imagining every moment of life as a story we are writing together with God.[1] This unique experience is possibly unlike any group in which you have participated. Whether a non-believer or longtime believer, you will learn more about God's story. Plus, you and your group will begin to see life as a place where God is active. The end result is learning to listen to God in our lives.

THE END

The end begins here. Any lasting life experience requires commitment to a paradigm outside the self and an end to selfishness. Most people on the planet choose to live almost exclusively centered upon the self. Decisions, purchases, and experiences are made because they bring some benefit for the self. People enter and abandon marriages, relationships, careers, and churches to achieve some personal satisfaction. However, for something to endure there needs to be a level of commitment beyond the self to some greater purpose. A marriage of two people, who only seek to fulfill personal needs, will end in two separate stories. When we realize the world is larger than the place where we stand, then we may accept the possibility of something other. This point of realization begins the end of individualism. Then, we may enter God's story.

This guidebook is a map. The destination is life with God. You and I, as reader and writer, become fellow travelers and conversation partners in sharing life together. The learning community we form illustrates

---

1. For more on cultivating a lifestyle of listening: Willard, *Hearing God*.

there is more to learn in life than one could ever understand alone. Our community begins a conversation and relationship with God. The discovery that something or someone is at work in human lives, long before they even realize it, is a slow process. Just as babies gradually become aware of the one feeding them and smiling at them, so human beings discover the larger story in which they participate unknowingly.

Let's start the journey! Get ready to tell some stories, listen to stories, and explore the connections of these stories. Who knows how our stories will reveal the activity of God? This invitation to the spiritual discipline of listening to others may transform us to hear echoes of something grand—a story that began before we were born and embraces us in love.

1

Week One: Narrating Life Together

Together we begin a journey through our everyday life stories into the story of God. Each week has four parts: one day to *Read* the story, one day to *Discuss* life in a small group, a *Practice* experience in listening for God during the week, and several days to *Reflect* on Scripture and life through readings and questions. This first week is a bit different because it introduces the whole process. This way you can read about it and then experience it. You will meet your group and get acquainted with the format for prayer and conversation.

DAY 1

▶READ

Everyone has a story. A story has everyone. These two phrases summarize the journey of this guidebook. The stories of people's lives show evidence of the larger story of God. Discovering this enormous story embracing us is shocking or even frustrating. It can feel like the man who hears a voice. In the movie, *Stranger than Fiction*, an uptight, meticulously ordered tax man named Harold Crick hears a voice in his head, narrating everything Harold does or even thinks. However, no one else hears the narrator's voice except Harold. He feels that he may be crazy so he visits a psychiatrist. Then he decides he's in a story and visits an English professor. Harold comes to believe his life is a story being written by someone else. Harold has a story, and a larger story embraces Harold. What might happen if we began to imagine our lives as creative participants in a large story?

Imagine life as story. A good story is worth sharing. Before we can hear God's story, we tell our own stories. This guidebook invites you into the intersection of divine and human stories. This process will help you draw connections between "your story" and "the story" of God. Discovering the story in which we live requires us to listen to other people's narratives and to learn to hear (and echo) the story of God.

This guidebook takes a small group of devoted believers through a process of listening to the story of God and then echoing the activity of God seen in the lives of others. This narrative experience includes four things each week: *reading* a summary of the story of God, participating in a small group *discussion, practicing* listening for echoes of God in everyday life, and *reflecting* deeply on Scripture and life.

This chapter prepares the leader and participants for this unique narrative process. This first week is different from the other chapters because it explains the process. So, treat this as a practice week to get familiar with the process. Specifically, this chapter explores some biblical passages about Jesus, the four elements of the catechesis structure are detailed as the Narrating Process, and the unique small group experience is explained in four moves.

Stories About Listening for Echoes of God

We enter a story with one primary attribute: listening. It is possible to live inside a story without ever listening to or reflecting on your story. However, to really engage a story one must listen. The experience of story requires that we imagine the world the story narrates. The virtue of listening is the beginning of understanding other people's narratives. Attentiveness to others and to God provides connections that weave them into a meaningful whole. Listening for echoes of God means noticing God's activity in everyday life. This process raises your awareness of God's activity. Here are two stories from the Bible about listening.

Two disciples of Jesus were discussing the events surrounding Jesus' death as they walked along. A stranger, who does not seem to know about the current events they are discussing, joins the pair of disciples. "What are you discussing with each other while you walk along?" asks the stranger named Jesus (Luke 24:17). His question does not give away his identity nor provide "the answer," but it invites them to talk about their experience of life. They stop dead in their tracks, look with surprise at Jesus, and ask if he is the only clueless person in Jerusalem (Luke

24:17–18). These disciples are likely a married couple, named Mary and Cleopas, who closely followed Jesus.[1] They know Jesus well but are kept from recognizing him. Jesus' question allows them to have the floor and to share what has happened from their perspective and experience. Jesus quietly listens.

It is interesting that Jesus chooses not to play the teacher. Jesus does not first instruct them systematically through the whole story of Scriptures why the Messiah must suffer, die, and be raised (Luke 24:27, 32). Jesus first listens to them. He asks another question, "What things?" and listens to things he already knows by firsthand experience, allowing them to talk and inform him. Jesus takes the humble posture of a listener. Then, after attentively listening to their stories, Jesus relates how the biblical story of God has room for a suffering servant. The result of Jesus' listening first is that they are held spellbound to his teaching about the story of God. They do not want him to leave. Hospitality is offered to those who listen first. Another instructive insight from this story is the moment of recognition. Jesus is identified at table fellowship as he prays. Within a safe, equal environment of sharing food, the divine is encountered in the midst of prayer. The whole process is informed by listening first.

There is another story encouraging listening and this one is about an enemy of Jesus. A man wanted to see Jesus and his disciples executed. While easily described as a terrorist, Saul was a religious man who killed others as an act of piety to God as he understood God. Saul could not hear Jesus narrating the story of God, until after Jesus died and came to visit him. Only then could Saul see Jesus as one with "beautiful feet," bringing the good news of God like Isaiah foretold (Isaiah 52:7). Later, Saul (now called Paul) writes from his personal experience that faith comes by hearing and hearing comes through the very words of Christ (Romans 10:17).

True listening for God develops our sense of hearing and our faith. When people listen for the echoes of God, they enter a story that sends them out into the world as proclaimers narrating of God's story. People are able to call on Jesus as Lord, when they believe. They believe when they hear, they hear when someone proclaims, and it is the proclaimers who are sent (Romans 10:13–15). The most important skill you will

---

1. Cleopas is mentioned by name here in Luke 15:18 and it is possible that the second person is his wife who was at the foot of the cross in John 19:25.

learn is how to listen to people for echoes of God. Listening means quietly observing, clarifying, and relating what the person communicates. Listening for echoes of God trains us in attentive observation of God's word on display in the lives of people.

The Narrating Process

Each week the guidebook leads you in four-part process of teaching people God's story from the Bible. The process provides participants opportunity to listen and echo God's story in everyday life. The four elements of this process—*reading* the chapter, *discussing* life in small group setting, *practicing* the art of echoing God in life's routine, and *reflecting* on spiritual readings—are detailed below.

▶ Read: The weekly reading section of the guidebook provides a chapter about the story of God. These chapters relate the story of the Bible from a bird's eye view. Scripture is narrated with a focus upon the activity of God and human response to God's action. The story of God is framed theologically. God is the creator who initiates covenant with humanity, makes promises, delivers promises, shows steadfast love, unites the world in Jesus, and leads humanity to the promised future. You are asked to read each chapter on your own time to begin the week. Each chapter is short and easily outlined by a few key points. At this altitude and at this pace, you will observe lots of content. While most stories are omitted, these stories are told to move readers through the ongoing plot of God's narrative. Content memorization is *not* our goal—we want to hear the stories. So, keep moving through the narrative and enjoy the background landscape of the biblical narrative. The highlight is observing life as a continuation of God's story.

▶ ▶ Discuss: The second element of the narrative process is a weekly sixty minute group experience. Each week a group of five to eight Christian adults will gather to share life and connect life to God's story. As the stories of life are narrated, the group may be surprised by the natural connections made with the story of God. This hour-long conversation is a hands-on experience that provides experience in the conversational art of sharing, listening, telling, and praying. In community our lives become the stage for God's story. Because of its importance, group discussion is dealt with more fully below in the next section of this chapter (p. 6).

▶ ▶ ▶ Practice: The third part of the process is a simple life exercise. It is unique, because it is practiced outside the safety of private study (reading the guidebook chapter or reflecting using the spiritual formation tool) and without the benefit of the group (the small group discussion time). Each week the leader gives an activity called "Echoes of God" to experiment the art of echoing God in life's routine. The echoes exercise prevents this from being just an intellectual study and turns it into shared experiment in the mission of God.

This first week the "Echoes of God" activity will be the practice of silence (p. 11). Obviously, in order to listen you must be silent. So, to prepare you to hear the story, you are asked to spend the next week living in as much silence as possible. Reduce your words. This is neither a silent retreat nor a vacation week. Simply go about your normal routine but enter silence by reducing the noise in your life and speaking less. First, turn off the iPod stereo, television, cell phone, and other noise-making media. This is a willing fast from some places and devices that fill life with sound. Second, do your best to speak only when necessary or when spoken to. Again, this week is not a vow of strict silence. You will need to talk at times, but do your best to limit speech. Each week, you will have a similar experiment to practice in your routine that will assist you in applying what is being learned from God's story, the stories of others, and your own story of faith. The group leader will remind you of this exercise at the end of the small group discussion.

▶ ▶ ▶ ▶ Reflect: Finally, all group members are strongly encouraged to reflect daily upon the story of God. This reflection involves reading some chapters from the Bible and using the spiritual formation reflection questions called "The Story & My Story." Each week has five days of Scripture readings. Learners may read either the long reading or the single chapter reading and then answer the two reflection questions. The first question deals with God from the Bible passage. The second question invites personal connection between the story of God and your story as the reader. Throughout the process, this spiritual formation tool allows you the opportunity to practice disciplines like Bible reading, prayer, study, journaling, and meditation. While the daily reading and reflection are not required, the learning experience is optimized with this spiritual reflection time.

Small Group Move One: Sharing Prayer

As promised, the next four headings explain the four moves in the small group discussion each week. The weekly small group conversation lasts sixty minutes. It begins with a unique prayer that is more than an opening prayer. The story of God is engaged through prayer. Many times prayer is used to start or quiet a group, and neither instance defines how prayer opens this process. Prayer enters us into the story of God. Humans bow before and address an eternal God. Prayer implies that the human story involves more than human activity.

The opening fifteen minute "Sharing Prayer" is more of a guided conversation that addresses God than it is a formal head bowed reciting of a prayer. Instead, the leader identifies this as a prayer with "open eyes," which bids each participant to address God with the group. There are four questions that people may answer. The questions may be taken one at a time, allowing the entire group to answer one, or participants may take turns answering all four questions. Some groups discover these four questions alone are enough to fill the discussion time with stories. Listening Leaders should simplify and adjust to what works best for your group.

The four parts of the prayer are thanksgiving, witnessing, confession, and intercession. The group leader asks the first sharing prayer question, "For what are you thankful?" Each willing participant replies, "I am thankful for . . ." and fills in the blank. This sharing responds to the invitation that gives gratitude to God. The second sharing question is "How have you witnessed God at work?" The reply begins, "I have seen God . . ." It is also possible to answer how one has seen "goodness" at work in the world, which is a helpful perspective when individuals are addressing non-believers or seekers. The same positive pointing to God takes place, but it is less threatening. The next sharing prayer question is "For what are you sorry?" Again, notice how each question invites participants to live in the story of God and assumes God works. This question invites prayerful reflection on our failure to live within God's story or even to live up to our personal definition of "goodness." Participants examine their lives and confess. The final question moves toward the mission of God. The leader asks, "Who needs to be shown love this week?" The short response "I am praying for" so-and-so imagines this individual in the context of the story of God. The prayer progresses from thanksgiving to God, on to awareness of God, into confession of inadequacy before God, and out to participation in God's mission of love.

This weekly ritual is a powerful experience, forming people to live by faith, voice hope, and be known by love.

Prayer begins our story experience as a response to God's activity in our lives. This sharing prayer should last about fifteen minutes and should promptly begin the gathering. The leader of sharing prayer is encouraged to pray silently to God as group participants share. The leader's prayer is not verbalized but is silent prayer of the heart. In this way, prayer permeates the small group conversation and life is directed toward God.

Small Group Move Two: Listening

This longest section lasts approximately thirty minutes and allows time for people to hear the stories of others. The leader invites the learners to listen and share stories of their life experiences with the group. One or two questions encourage participants to tell a story from their life. The listening section of the small group contains questions and statements that invite stories from group members. The question relates to the chapter reading about the story of God, prior to the gathering. The aim is to generate an open conversational storytelling time each week among the group. Listening leaders should feel free to develop questions to fit their unique group.

Once again, prayer covers this process. The leader still is praying silently for the members of the group, as they share their story. Prayers may be offered for those struggling to tell their story. A prayer of celebration may be offered for someone who shares an especially revealing story from the past. The leader listens to the stories for echoes of God's activity, which will be narrated in the discussion's next step.

Small Group Move Three: Telling

The third move is telling (or echoing) the story. During this part, the Listening Leader narrates the story of God based upon the evening's conversation. This allows the leader to show that he or she has been carefully listening to the experiences of the entire group. In order to narrate the story of God, the Listening Leader draws upon their advanced reading of the chapter, Scripture, the constant prayers they have offered to God for participants, and their attentiveness to the stories of those in the group.

Typically a theme emerges in the stories shared. As people tell stories, the stories connect to one another. By listening to the stories of others, people are transformed. The leader listens for reoccurring words or themes in the discussion. Then, the leader verbalizes (echoes) these insights to the group in this move. During this time, the Listening Leader might draw upon a Bible story from the reading or an insight gained from the guidebook chapter. The leader also might think of a different passage of Scripture to impart a word from God into the conversation. Often the passage comes to mind in the constant prayer during the sharing and listening moves. If no passage comes to mind, the Listening Leader might ask if anyone has a passage or biblical story to share that connects the conversations.

This conversation lasts for approximately ten minutes and it links the reading, prayer time, and story-listening time. Here the leader echoes the activity of God by repeating the story of God as it connects with the group's life experiences. Sometimes these connections are made by discussing a passage (as mentioned above). Other times a leader might make broad connections to God as creator, covenant-maker, covenant-keeper, or deliverer. These may be roles that God is playing in the lives of the participants.

In Luke 24, Jesus takes an encounter with the two disciples on the Emmaus road and uses it for teaching. Jesus reveals truth from the Law of Moses and the writings of the Prophets that further enhance their understanding of Jesus as Lord and Messiah. A similar echoing of Scripture in life experience is practiced by the Listening Leader of the group discussion. The narrating of life leads to the narrating of the story of God, which often results in a life-changing perspective on life.

Small Group Move Four: Connecting Prayer

Finally, the leader moves the group into connecting prayer. This prayer has both formal and spontaneous elements. First, the group bows and joins the leader in reciting Solomon's prayer: "O Lord, God of Israel, there is no God like you in heaven above or on earth beneath, keeping covenant and steadfast love for your servants who walk before you with all their heart" (1 Kings 8:23). Then, the leader prays an impromptu prayer that draws upon the conversations of sharing, listening, and narrating from the entire discussion. Once again, prayer enters us into the story of God. This connecting prayer is an invitation to allow God to carry the conversation forward into action in life. There is no formula needed for this prayer other than to recognize God is at work in the lives of people, address the stories of the participants, and petition God to remain at work in the coming week. The gathering closes by being surrounded in prayer in God's presence. From the opening sharing prayer through the listening and narrating of stories, prayer has been the arena to echo God's activity in life.

The group *Discuss* process of sharing, listening, narrating, and connecting resembles the moves of the prayerful spiritual practice of *Lectio Divina* or "sacred reading" of Scripture. *Lectio Divina* is a contemplative method of reading and praying Scripture that has four parts: reading (*lectio*), listening (*meditatio*), speaking (*oratio*), and connecting (*contemplatio*). In *Lectio Divina*, Scripture is first read aloud (*lectio*) in repetitive fashion and then a word or phrase becomes the focus of the heart (*meditatio*). The meaningful word or phrase then becomes a prayer offered to God (*oratio*). Finally, the reader dwells in the presence of God in contemplation (*contemplatio*). The process of narrative catechesis uses the human life as a text for the practice of *Lectio Divina*. The group reads from life (sharing or *lectio*) and then listens to the stories of others (listening or *meditatio*). Next, the leader narrates a comparison to the story of God (*oratio*). Finally, the group prays a connecting prayer drawing attention to God's presence (*contemplatio* or connecting). *Lectio Divina* offers an interesting correlation to the practice of echoing God's activity.

> **LEADER PREP:**
>
> Familiarize yourself with the process by re-reading the Introduction chapter and this chapter.

This chapter described the process of formation that will take place using the narrative catechesis guidebook. It will demand your prayerful spiritual attention over the next several weeks (leaders may read this chapter again). Participation in reading the chapter, conversation in the small group, practicing the echoes of God activity, and reflecting daily with the spiritual formation tool will be demanding but enriching as you prepare to hear and echo God's activity.

Day 2

▷▶ DISCUSS

Small Group Discussion (60 minutes)

The small group is a time of story telling bookended with prayer. The Sharing Prayer is an exercise that allows people to share experiences from their week yet focus them upon God. The Connecting Prayer draws together the stories from the evening and again offers them to God. God's story is the focus throughout this process. The two center moves (Move 2 and Move 3) are laidback story sharing time. This is not a typical "Bible Study" or topical small group. Instead, we listen and tell stories from life while watching for hints of God. So, grab a comfy pillow or lean back on your sofa and enjoy the surprise of observing the ways God is working in our lives.

> **LEADER:**
> Begin by asking people to introduce themselves and tell why they came. Then, overview the process for the group briefly. Remember this first week is different and more like a trial run of the small group *Discussion*.

MOVE 1: *SHARING* PRAYER CONVERSATION (15 MINUTES)

- For what are you *thankful*? (Thanksgiving to God)
- How have you seen *God at work*? (Witnessing God)
- For what are you *sorry*? (Confession to God)
- To whom do you need to *show love*? (Mission of God)

MOVE 2: *LISTENING* TO OTHERS' STORIES (30 MINUTES)

- Share an event, movie, song, hobby, or passion that in some way expresses your identity.
- Tell a story of when you were surprised to discover that more was going on than you realized (surprise party, secret award, unexpected divorce, etc.).
- What has been your relationship with the Bible? Read Luke 24:13–35.

Move 3: *Telling* Stories (10 minutes)

- The Listening Leader reflects connections between the stories told in the Sharing and Listening times with the story of God in the reading or Scripture.
- For example, the Leader could summarize how the Luke 24 passage can make us expectant for God to show up in these next weeks.

> **Leader:**
> This "telling" move is an opportunity to connect (echo) a story of God with stories people shared. Each week in this section you will summarize group conversations in light of the story of God (p. 7).

Move 4: *Connecting* Conversation Prayer (5 minutes)

- This prayer time begins by reciting 1 Kings 8:23 together:

   O Lord, God of Israel, there is no God like you
   in heaven above or on earth beneath,
   keeping covenant and steadfast love
   for your servants who walk before you with all their heart.

- Leader offers a prayer that reflects some of the stories and conversations from the group discussion.

> **Leader:**
> Before dismissing the group, explain the Echoes of God activity (see *Practice* below) to the group. Encourage participation so people can practice listening for echoes of God.

Days 3—7

▷▷▶PRACTICE

Echoes of God Activity

This week practice the discipline of silence. Reduce the noise in your life by avoiding media (television, music, radio, movies, etc.). Also, attempt to conserve words by being as silent as possible. Why silence? Well, if we are to learn the skill of "listening" for God a great place to begin is by listening to others. Become aware of God's Story as you listen for echoes of God's activities in the ordinary places of life. This requires that you intentionally place yourself out in the world as a witness of God's activity. Come ready to share how God instructed you through this listening exercise.

▷▷▷▶ REFLECT

This first week does not have daily readings from Scripture or reflection questions—these begin next week. Instead, focus on the Echoes of God activity of silence, review the process described in this chapter, reread the Luke 24 passage, and prayerfully anticipate God's activity in your life this week.

2

Week Two: God Creates a Covenant People

This week we engage the story of God. First *Read* the chapter before your small group gathering. The reading provides one telling of God's story as background. Then engage in the group *Discuss* experience of listening and sharing. Likely you will be surprised at how God is working in others' lives and in yours, too. Next, take note of the Echoes of God experiment to help you *Practice* listening for God's activity. Finally, *Reflect* daily on some passages in the story of God and on your own journey of faith.

DAY 1

▶ READ

Once beyond time there was God, and "in the beginning God created the heavens and the earth." We humans were not there. This story begins with its main character: God. It is a story of God's action as seen through human experience over thousands of years. The Christian faith is grounded in a good news story. Rather than simply being a religious source book of instructions and codes, the Bible is full of stories that guide the narrative. This is unique among other world religions, which instruct. God has the lead role. The Bible presents the relationship story of God's pursuit of humankind.

This chapter tells three stories about God and three people. These three stories reveal three important things about God. God is a creator. God is a promise maker. God is a deliverer. God's action is always primary, because God acts before human beings. Humans respond to God by receiving what God gives, ignoring God, or worshiping God.

First, God creates. "In the beginning God created." After six days of poetic creation, the Book of Genesis brings us to God's highest handiwork: the human being created from dirt. The climax of God's creation is the human being. The human being is made in the image of God (Gen 1:1, 26–27). No other part of creation is given this god-like identity. Humans are fantastic in God's eyes. You can look in the mirror and see Adam and Eve. Within our bodies is the God-given genetic DNA passed down through the ages from Adam and Eve.

Humans are family. We have different skin tone, eye color, hair thickness, and language; but, we are all made in God's image. The separation of race, geography, culture, or politics does not erase that we are part of God's human family. In times of war and peace, we would do well to remember our relationship. While in our country's recent history, we had separate bus seats and drinking fountains, we are brothers and sisters with all humanity. On the inside we bleed the same red blood, have the same white bones, and the same yellow fat. And when we die, each of our bodies eventually returns to the same black dirt from which we came. We are family created by God.

Things begin in Eden, a garden positioned somewhere in Iraq. The Tigris and Euphrates Rivers found in Iraq are mentioned in Genesis 2. This place of modern war once was paradise. In the Garden of Eden, God makes an agreement with his created people. God provides food for us. Humans are to care for the earth as a garden. Humans are to avoid the tree of knowledge. This forbidden tree holds the fruit of the knowledge of good and evil. In the story, this tree is a place of moral awareness. Good and evil may be defined by individual choice, rather than God.

The whole story is powerfully symbolic, poetic, and revealing. "Adam," the name of the first man literally means "earth." Adam names "Eve," which means "mother of living." A snake entices Adam and Eve to eat fruit from the tree of moral knowledge saying, "Surely God cannot be trusted. God is worried about losing power." The temptation is for humans to become "like God" through their own effort, to determine good and evil on their own. Knowledge of good and evil is given, but this fruit does not give life or god-like status. God already made us in God's image. The snake deceives humanity. Human naïveté is lost. Humans are exposed as displacers of God.

It never takes long before disobedience enters our lives. When my son Nathan was learning to crawl, we decided it was time to teach our speechless infant the word "no." A large peace lily plant sat on the floor. It intrigued Nathan. He wanted to touch the plant. We would tell him "no" and move him away from the plant. This became a game for him. He, like every person, was learning the knowledge of good and evil, developing moral awareness. Some things are good. Some things are evil. Most everything in the house was good. The peace lily was "evil." He would crawl toward the plant and look up at us and smile. We would say "no" and move him away. He would crawl towards it and grab hold of a leaf, and we would pull him away. Nathan began to learn "no" and not to mess with the plant. Those things we say "no" to are most interesting. We called the plant "The Tree of Knowledge of Good and Evil." Eventually, he would crawl toward the plant, knowing we were watching. Then, he would sit right up next to the pot with the plant's leaves around his body like a coat and hat. This is a fact of human nature: we test the limits. We want those things we cannot have.

In the beginning, God created humans. We wanted to play the role of God and we failed. God looked for these hiding people, asking, "Where are you?" This question is still one we must answer. Where are we in relationship to God? Our actions force God to judge us. We are created. We are called to do good and live with God. Our actions have consequences. God removed us from the plant and from the Garden of Eden.

Notice that the death God promised is not instantaneous. Death becomes a new reality in human existence. We are born. We die. All humanity shares the realities of birth and death. Even in punishment of removal from paradise, God is gracious and merciful. Death is delayed. The clothes made by God cover the nakedness of an exposed humanity. God is loving and merciful with his children.

The second move of the story is how God covenants with humanity through two characters: Abram and Sarai. What is a covenant? I'm glad you asked. A covenant or promise is an expression of willingness to do something. God makes a promise to Abram and Sarai. Abram does not ask for these blessings, God simply gives these blessings. No one forces God to make this promise. No one says, "Do you swear by God?" As if God had to say, "I swear by myself." God takes initiative and makes a promise with humanity. A covenant is a binding oath within an ongoing relationship. God created us. We did not create ourselves. God chose us and maintains the promise of relationship.

In Genesis 12:1–13, the eternal creator God promises to make Abram into a great nation. Abram is chosen of all the people in the world (and of all the people who have *ever* lived) to be first in a special group. The ancestors of Abram are children of promise/covenant, "set apart" (or holy) as God's priests to the entire world. God promises four important things: to make Abram into a nation of people, to give him land, to bless Abram and his people, and to bless every nation of the earth through Abram.

A promise is not a law. God does not establish a law with Abram. God creates relationship with humans in covenant. God takes the initiative. The promise depends upon God. The law, specifically the "Law of Moses," comes much later . . . 430 years later. God's promise comes first. That is significant and teaches us something about God as an eternal parent. God's promise to us comes before God's law for us.

We make promises to a friend, boss, spouse, parent, or child. In Abram's time, there were different types of covenant promises. Three covenant types are especially interesting. One was a promise made between two equals, like brother to brother. This agreement bound them together in a relationship of mutual respect and friendship. This was a peer-to-peer covenant. Second, there was a covenant between a king and a subject, like a boss-to-employee relationship. The boss was given absolute sovereignty over the employees. In return, the employee gave his loyalty and service. This was an ongoing relationship. As long as the employee was trustworthy, then the boss would pay and give him health care. A third type of covenant is a grant, which a ruler makes with a citizen. It is like winning the lottery. A citizen is given a thank-you gift. This third type of covenant is like the one God makes with Abraham. God grants Abraham identity and protection.

The significance of this promise made by God with Abram is huge. God makes promises to Abraham, which he did not have to make. Most importantly, the covenant promise is prior to the law, which came 430 years later, and was superior to law. In Galatians 3:17–18, Paul explains the primary place of the promise:

> My point is this: the law, which came four hundred thirty years later, does not annul a covenant previously ratified by God, so as to nullify the promise. For if the inheritance comes from the law, it no longer comes from the promise; but God granted it to Abraham through the promise. (See also Galatians 3:6–9)

The entire story of God is written on the premise that God creates the world and makes a promise to the world through Abram. This promise is the lens to understand human history for Jews, Christians, and outsiders—not the law. This promise continues a grand narrative of good news.

There is a problem with the promise. Abram has no children. Abram is a homeless nomad. God's promise does not come true quickly. In fact, God makes the promise over and over again, but nothing happens. Abram and Sarai just get older.

When God first makes the promise in Genesis 12, he asks a 75-year-old Abram to pack up everything for an unknown journey to an unknown land. God makes the promise again, and Abram builds an altar to God (12:7). A third time God promises Abram's descendants will be like dust (13:14-17). There is still no answer. A fourth promise comes in chapter 15. Abram bows humbly and says, "God you have given me nothing." God lifts Abram's chin out of the dust to look up at the stars, telling him to count the stars to know the number of his children. Still waiting in chapter 16, Abram and Sarai decide to help God. Sarai "loans" her female servant to her husband. Their sexual relationship creates a child, Ishmael, but he is not the promised child. The Bible is full of imperfect people who are not examples. God does not need heroes but makes heroes out of dirt.

In chapter 17, Abram is now 99 years old. It has been almost twenty-five years of waiting for God to come through. This is now the same song fifth verse. God promises to give Abram many children. This fifth promise is the first time God asks Abram to follow him with all his heart. God's promise is still primary, but now the promise makes a claim on Abram's lifestyle. Children of promise live differently.

Abram literally means "exalted father." God changes his name to Abra*ham*, which means ironically "father of nations." Surely God has a sense of humor. Then, God asks this "dad of multitudes" to take a knife to his private parts as a sign of the covenant (circumcision). Abraham, the father of nobody at this point, is to cut the foreskins around the men's penises to show that he will follow God. God's demands are razor sharp. Abraham laughs out loud at the thought of giving birth through Sarai, who is nearly as old as he is.

Sarai also receives a name change. Both of these spellings of her name mean the same thing "princess." Her new spelling is a less archaic spelling, but most importantly is the description of Sarah as a princess who will "give rise to the nations" and "kings of people will come from her" (Genesis 17:17). Conception is always God's gift at any age.

In a sixth visit, God comes in the physical form of a human being who promises that Sarah will give birth next year (Genesis 18:18–19). This time Sarah laughs. Finally, at 100 years old, the father of multitudes holds a child born of his wife Sarah (v. 21). After twenty-five years of waiting, and seven visits from God, the promise is born as new life. God is truly hilarious. The name of the promised child is "Isaac," which means "he laughs" or, as I love to say, little "Hilarious." The covenant to Abraham blesses all people.

As generations pass from Abraham's time, God forgets his people and his covenant with them. Overnight it seems they became slaves instead of guests in Egypt. God falls asleep. But, God hears desperate cries of slaves. God sees their misery. God knows the ancestors of Abraham are suffering (Exodus 1:7–8) so God comes down. In the mysterious flame of a bush, God calls a leader named Moses. His name means not "the one who draws out" but "drawn out," pointing to God as the one who draws Moses out of water and also draws his people through water. God is the one who delivers his created and chosen people. This prince turned shepherd questions his own ability. Moses wants to know the identity of the God of Abraham. God says, "I am what I am." The divine name Yahweh means "I will be what I will be."

With God's name on his lips, the fire of God in his heart, and the staff of God in his hand, Moses follows the deliverer God Yahweh right into Egypt. After ten havoc-wreaking plagues over a period of almost one year, millions of Hebrews were set free one night. They cross through the river of the Red Sea. Something powerful happened in those years with Moses. The Exodus story provides a Hebrew identity of a people following Yahweh God, the deliverer. Nothing could stop Yahweh—not powerful pharaoh kings, natural disasters, or physical boundaries. God reigns.

God's people return to the mountain of the burning bush and are given the Ten Commandments. They are given food. They are presented with land. But for the most part they grumble, complain, doubt leadership, and long for slavery. The result is years of wandering in the desert. They wait for a generation of people to die off and a younger generation to receive the land God promised.

Their story is still our story today: God creates us, God makes covenant with us, and God delivers us. The story of God forms the lens of our reality, a way of seeing the large story that defines us. God created you and is your source of origin. God makes a covenant promise with us, even though we are imperfect. God's promise invites us to create life with him and participate in his work. However, our attempts at creation and living in God's promises sometimes go unfulfilled. Sometimes it seems God has forgotten or delayed the covenant and at other times we (or Adam or Abraham or Moses) break the covenant. Still, we continue trusting the presence and word of God to deliver us. God must complete what he started in us as he promised us. This is a movement of faith: we are created, we are invited into relationship, we break relationship, and we look to God for deliverance. You are invited to connect your personal life story to this story of God. Trust God as the maker of your past, the protector of your future, and your present guide. Live this story.

Day 2

▷▶ DISCUSS

Small Group Discussion (60 minutes)

This week the group dives into the Story of God. Make sure to read the above reading "God Creates a Covenant People" prior to the group gathering as it will help you make connections with the story of God. The small group format should become more familiar to you over the next few weeks. If you were not able to do all the readings and reflection last week do not worry. Just pick up and begin reading with this week.

> **LEADER:**
>
> Prior to the small group meeting become comfortable with the *Read* material. In the *Telling* move you will tie the group's stories to the story of God.

Move 1: Sharing Prayer Conversation (15 minutes)

- For what are you *thankful*?
- How have you *seen God at work* this week?
- For what are you *sorry*?
- To whom do you *need to show love*?

> **LEADER:**
>
> Begin on time. Allow the opening *Sharing* time to be a lively conversational prayer. These questions are a great way to spiritually frame our week in light of God. Some groups find these four questions are enough to fill a sixty minute group discussion.

MOVE 2: *LISTENING TO OTHERS' STORIES* (30 MINUTES)

- Describe your experience of silence last week in the first the Echoes of God activity.
- Share a significant time in your life when someone made or broke a promise to you. Consider a time when someone kept a promise that they did not have to keep.

MOVE 3: *TELLING STORIES* (10 MINUTES)

- The Listening Leader articulates connections between the stories people told in the session about promises and the story of God from the reading or Scripture.
- For example, reflect back to the group some comments or stories shared in the Sharing and Listening moves. Make associations between the groups experiences of promise and the story of a God who creates us, makes commitments to us, and will deliver us.

MOVE 4: *CONNECTING CONVERSATION PRAYER* (5 MINUTES)

- This prayer time begins by reciting 1 Kings 8:23 together:

    O Lord, God of Israel, there is no God like you
    in heaven above or on earth beneath,
    keeping covenant and steadfast love
    for your servants who walk before you with all their heart.

- Leader ends with a prayer that reflects some of the stories and conversations from the group discussion.

> **LEADER:**
>
> Before dismissing the group, explain the Echoes of God activity (see *Practice* below) to the group. Encourage participation so people can practice listening for echoes of God.

Days 3—7

▷▷▶ PRACTICE

Echoes of God Activity

This week make a promise to someone and keep it. Listen throughout the week for promises that other people make and keep or make and break.

▷▷▷▶ REFLECT

The Story & My Story

These Scripture readings and questions are for reflection. The first question deals with the text and the second with "My Story." If you have less time read only the underlined chapter.

Day 3: Genesis 1–2, <u>12</u>–15

- How is God's grace seen in his promises to Adam and Abraham?
- Do I want more to *be blessed* by others or to *be a blessing* to others?

> **PARTICIPANTS:**
> Remember the Echoes activity. Have you noticed some promises made? Have you made a promise and kept it?

Day 4: Exodus 1, <u>2</u>, 3, 4

- What is significant to you about God "remembering his people?"
- When has God remembered me when I thought he had forgotten?

Day 5: Exodus 19–<u>20</u>, Leviticus 16, 17

- What does the order of the Ten Commandments show about God's character?
- Am I more concerned with keeping appearances or with honoring God with my life?

Day 6: Numbers 11–14

- Describe God's relationship with his people.
- How has God provided for me?

Day 7: Read Deuteronomy 5–7

- Why does God choose this particular people?
- How does it affect me to know that God chose me?

> **PARTICIPANTS:**
> Tomorrow you begin next week's readings. So, read the Week Three *Read* section prior to your group meeting. Take a moment to reflect or journal about your experience with the Echoes of God activity.

3

Week Three: God Rules and Pursues His People

The story of God continues in our lives. First, *Read* the chapter the day before your small group gathering. Remember you do not have to master this content. This tells God's story from Scripture. Then, meet with your group to *Discuss* and experience how listening and sharing stories can focus upon God. Next, consider (*Practice*) the Echoes of God activity to open your ears to God's work in life. Finally, spend time daily *Reflecting* on Scripture passages and connecting them with your journey of faith.

Day 1

▶ READ

We are living out the story of our lives. We co-author a story that God began. The Bible tells the overarching narrative of God. Approaching the Bible as an ongoing story of God, gives believers and non-believers, insiders and outsiders to Christianity, a healthy look at life from God's view.

Christians believe in a God who created the world and gives us life. We trust the God who makes relationship through a covenant promise with a specific people for the benefit of every living thing. While at times the creator God seems absent in keeping the world going right, we admit that humans often make a mess of this world. However, we believe God will deliver people from oppression in time.

One abiding question humans wrestle with is this: "Who is in charge?" In the work place or home life, there are questions on authority. Sometimes authority is clear. I have worked for many bosses: the District Attorney of the largest county in Colorado (Jefferson), a criminal manager at Wendy's who tried to set me up as a thief, a drunken real estate appraiser, and more. Some people let God be boss. Others refuse to believe in anything bigger than the self and retain control of their lives. Some religious people claim God's authority yet live as they please. Some deny God and live as they desire.

God rules humanity and continually pursues relationship with us. You may notice every chapter title of this book communicates this important truth, because each title begins with God. God is our origin. These titles state how God seeks relationship with humanity. Following God as a wandering nomad (Abraham) in a tent looks different than people settled in houses in the promised land (Joshua). This chapter looks at two more ways God leads his people: through the law and through human leaders.

The story of God from the Bible does not begin with a law code: "In the beginning were the rules." Rather, the Bible is a story of God's relationship with people. Over the thousands of years of history interpreted in the Bible, God's covenant relationship is primary. The most famous and most important covenant of the Bible is the one God made to Abram. God promised to bless Abram with offspring, land, and relationship with God and the world. The blessed and wealthy Abram is an example of God blessing those who walk with God. However, *God's blessing is not an exclusive blessing for Abraham but an inclusive blessing for humanity.* All humanity qualifies as children of God and heirs to this promise. God does not play favorites or show partiality.

The people God chooses are given responsibility to live in God's blessings. But how does this happen? The Law of Moses is given to the Hebrew people. This vast group of people was enslaved to Egypt. Evidently the distinction "Hebrew," or what other ancient texts may call *Habiru*, was not a racial or national identity but a nonspecific social class of nomadic people.[1] God's impartiality is clear in choosing a loosely connected group of travelers. God created humanity, entered relationship with Abraham, delivered the Hebrews through Moses, and now this diverse people need direction.

The Law of Moses given on Mount Sinai or Mount Horeb provided direction. Most people have heard of the Ten Commandments, the memorable summary of the Law of Moses. These and other command-

---

1. Redmount, "Bitter Lives: Israel in and out of Egypt," 97–98.

ments are found in Bible's first five books, called the Pentateuch, which means five.

The Hebrew word for "law" is *torah*, which literally means "pointing" and "instruction." Imagine the law as a giant finger that points back to the covenant promise given to Abraham. Imagine this giant finger also points forward to the way of living with God in covenant. We humans need "pointing" in the right direction. We need instructive guidance on how we should live. The law points to following God.

People fail to recognize the important difference between promise and law. A law is different from a promise. A promise is like this: "I promise to buy you lunch." A law is more like this: "You must eat a sandwich on a plate at noon." The law is a servant to its master, the covenant. God first makes promises. Then, God points to the promise through law. This significant distinction indicates that God puts priority on relationship with humans over rules. God enters relationship first and then gives direction about that relationship.

Believers often overemphasize the law and underemphasize relationship. Laws are intended to keep people from harming one another—do not murder, do not steal, do not take someone else's spouse, take care of your family. These rules are basics for relationship. The Ten Commandments are foundational for any law code. Sometimes humans use laws to destroy relationship by giving law priority over people.

However, the Ten Commandments begin in relationship! The first commandment begins inside God's story. God says, "Remember I am the Lord your God who brought you out of Egypt and out of slavery, so worship me only" (Exodus 20:2–3; Deuteronomy 5:6–7). Remember these laws come from a story written in God's mercy. This nomadic group of freed slaves has a unique religion, worshiping one God. Monotheism was unique in ancient times when many gods were worshiped (paganism). The second command forbids making idols, statues, or images of God. God cannot be contained in one image.

The Ten Commandments begin in relationship to God (first four commands) and end in relationship to others (last six). The law helps us live the covenant relationship. But, the law is neither God nor savior. The promises and laws reveal God's salvation.

God pursues relationship and leads people with law. The law is one method of ruling people. God also presents leaders to rule his people. Abraham first lived in relationship with God. From his descendants

God selects leaders like Moses, Aaron, and Joshua, who provide God-following leadership.

Moses is probably the greatest leader in the Bible other than Jesus. This deliverer and prophet with a face-to-face relationship with God is credited with assembling the Pentateuch. Moses is about to die or as the Bible puts it "go the way of dirt." The people want to know who is in charge. Joshua inherits the leadership of Moses. That must have been incredibly intimidating for Joshua. In the opening to the Book of Joshua, God commands Joshua to be strong, courageous, and obedient (Joshua 1:6–9). God promises his presence with Joshua in the same way he was present with Moses (1:5). Joshua is responsible to lead the people to the land promised to their ancestors, the "Promised Land." While Joshua is the leader, the Law of Moses lives up to its name and "points" Joshua and the people to the promises of Abraham. They are pointed to victory and pointed to a new homeland by God's leading.

The conquest of the land was God's accomplishment. God never gave up even when the people were afraid to take this gift. Joshua lived by the law. In the closing chapters of Joshua's book, Joshua assembles all of the twelve tribes at Shechem. He commands the removal of the idols (23:14–16) and obedience to God. The issue remains: "who is in charge?" Joshua leads the people to God. Good leaders follow God. Bad leaders have many celebrity idols they follow which distract from God's leadership. These idols, whether visible or invisible, entice people to live opposed to God's story.

Often leaders have some phrase for which they are known. In the book's last chapter, Joshua's famous statement is posed. Joshua says, "Choose for yourselves who you will serve" whether this god or that god, "but as for me and my household we will serve Yahweh, the Lord" (24:15). Joshua will not serve many gods, because for him only one God is leader. The people are inspired. They intend not to forsake Yahweh, because he saved them from slavery and gave them the land. Everyone is now on the same page, but Joshua throws cold water on their response. He says they will be unable to serve God because of their unfaithfulness. Yahweh God is far too holy, and they are too rebellious. They insist Yahweh will rule. Joshua sets up a large stone under an oak tree near the holy place of the Lord as a reminder of their choice to serve Yahweh alone.

As Joshua dies, the people first ask, "Who is in charge of leading us into battle?" (Judges 1:1). Again, the crowds want a leader to provide direction. Yahweh the Lord is the one who answers the call. So, God provides judges in response to the people's cries. The book of Judges describes the rise of a judge confederacy. These men and women are appointed by God to guide the people in the ways of God. Four things distinguish these judges. They are charismatic leaders, guided by the spirit of God. These military leaders battle foes like the Canaanites. Third, the judges make judicial decisions. Finally, judges do not rule over the whole nation but over sections of people. Unlike a solitary king, multiple judges rule at the same time. There are many more than the twelve recorded in Judges.

The basic storyline of Judges is played like a rerun in our lives. There is a cycle of the judge's leadership (2:18–22). The cycle begins in *silent* need of leadership. Next, comes a time of *sinfulness* and chaos followed by a period of *suffering* and difficulty. This causes the people to cry out to God in *supplication*. Finally, *salvation* arrives when God sends a judge. So the five-part cycle is a drama that includes: silence with a judge's death, sinfulness of the people, suffering punishment, petitions from the people, and then salvation with a new judge.

Gideon is a memorable judge. God directs Gideon to an unorthodox military victory using a few soldiers armed with clay pots and fire torches. After that astounding victory, the people want to appoint Gideon to "rule over them." Instead, Gideon's one liner defines his leadership, "I will not rule over you, and my son will not rule over you; The Lord will rule over you" (Judges 8:22–23). Gideon knows who is in charge. The best leaders do not serve their own interests. The best leaders do not flaunt credentials. The best leaders follow God. Ironically, in the entire book of Judges, the noun form "judge" is used only twice. In the Hebrew, the title "judge" is used for God, "Let the Lord, who is judge, decide" (Judges 11:27). Outside the introduction, the remainder of the judges are said to have "judged," but the title "judge" is given to God.

There are hints of the next phase of God's leadership through a repeated refrain in Judges: "There was no king in all Israel; all the people did what was right in their own eyes" (17:6; 18:1; 19:1; 21:25). The implication of having no singular leader is that everything is mayhem, because people are self-directed. Each person does what they think is best. So, God sends a monarchy at the people's request. The people of

Israel grow tired of having no clear visible leader and ask for a king. Samuel is a judge and prophet who speaks on God's behalf. While a great leader, Samuel is aging. He tries appointing his sons, but they are evil and the people refuse. The idea of a monarchy angers Samuel, because it rejects God as king. So, Samuel does what any good leader does. He prays (1 Samuel 8:4–9). God explains how the people have rejected the leadership of God and not that of Samuel. When people ask, "Who is in charge," believers always answer "God" but few ever actually seek and submit to God.

The monarchy of Israel is best remembered for three kings: Saul, David, and Solomon. The first God-appointed king is an extremely shy giant of a man, who eventually sets covenant aside (1 Sam 15:10-11). Samuel is forced to tell King Saul that the kingdom will be ripped from his hand and given to another.

Next, God anoints the head of David as king, the most beloved king in the history of the Jews. He is a handsome, powerful military leader, poetic song writer, and devoted to God. He is also sinful. His sexual exploits and murder conspiracy get him into trouble. However, unlike King Saul, David is always repentant. David is a man after God's own heart, because David seeks God's heart. Unfortunately, as David takes a woman not his wife, so Israel takes lovers other than God.

Third, David's son, Solomon, ascends the throne. David commissions Solomon's faithful living before God (1 Kings 2:2-4). However, Solomon turns his focus to other gods. Marrying wives from the surrounding kingdoms, Solomon inherits the gods or idols belonging to his wives (1 Kings 11:1-4). Not one of these three kings is perfect. The Bible is not about perfect people or heroes. The Bible is about how God works through weakness, calling people to his leadership. Consider who is in charge of your life. Leaders come and go, but God's lordship remains permanent. The story of God is a theocracy (not a single leader, a judge, or a king). Each of us is ruled by idols or kings rather than God. Often we worry more about church issues, a governmental party, the accumulation of dollars, or the security of peace than setting our heart on following God.

In the story of God, the question to be asked is not "Who is in charge?" but "Who will follow?" Who is willing to follow God completely? Trust the future to God. Choose this day to serve God and be a leader in following the Lord.

Day 2

▷▶ DISCUSS

Small Group Discussion (60 minutes)

The discussion time forms a pretty simple ritual that becomes more and more familiar. The simple structure creates space for people to share their stories of life and locate their stories within the story of God.

Move 1: Sharing Prayer Conversation (15 minutes)

- For what are you *thankful*?
- How have you *seen God at work*?
- For what are you *sorry*?
- To whom do you *need to show love*?

> **Leader:**
> The opening prayer time may begin to feel familiar. You might mention this prayer is similar to Saint Ignatious' 'Prayer of Examen' and may be used daily for personal reflection. When leaders start on time they help members learn to arrive on time.

Move 2: Listening to Others' Stories (30 minutes)

- Share some stories about promises from last week's "Echoes of God" experience.
- Tell about a significant person in your life as you grew up.
- Tell about an event from childhood that gave you purpose or meaning.

> **Leader:**
> Sometimes writing a few notes about the stories or comments people share will help you connect people to the story of God. Briefly highlight some of the connections made in the *Telling* move.

Move 3: Telling Stories (10 minutes)

- The Listening Leader articulates connections between the stories told in the session and the story of God from the reading or Scripture.
- For example, the leader may highlight some similarities between group members and biblical characters or other significant people

mentioned. Connect Moses with someone adopted, Joshua with someone taking a new job, Gideon with a reluctant person, and David with an unlikely leader.

Move 4: Connecting Conversation Prayer (5 minutes)

- This prayer time begins by reciting 1 Kings 8:23 together:

    O Lord, God of Israel, there is no God like you
    in heaven above or on earth beneath,
    keeping covenant and steadfast love
    for your servants who walk before you with all their heart.

- Leader ends with a prayer that reflects some of the stories and conversations from the group discussion.

> **Leader:**
> Before dismissing the group, describe the Echoes of God activity below. Encourage group members to practice listening this week.

Days 3—7

▷▷▶ PRACTICE

Echoes of God Activity

This week listen to how people talk about their bosses and other people in authority. Notice of whether what is said is more positive or more negative. Keep a scorecard to see whether positive or negative comments win.

▷▷▷▶ REFLECT

The Story & My Story

These Scripture readings and questions are for daily reflection. Question one reflects on the text and the second on "My Story." If you have less time read only the underlined chapter.

Day 3: Joshua <u>1</u>–2, 6, 23, 24

- In what ways does God lead the Hebrew people?
- How does (should) God lead my life?

Day 4: Judges 1, 2, 3, 4

- What do you learn about God's patience and faithfulness from this reading?
- In what ways am I unable to learn from past mistakes?

Day 5: 1 Samuel 16, 17, 18, 19

- What is the difference between Saul and David's view of God?
- What one thing do I need to allow God to conquer for me?

Day 6: 2 Samuel 7, 9, 11, 12

- Where does God live?
- How do I limit God to a particular place?

> **REMINDER:**
> The Echoes of God activity this week has you listening for conversations about authority figures (like bosses, politicians, or parents). Notice how people talk about those in power in their lives.

Day 7: 1 Kings 1, 2, 3, 4

- What is important about David's advice to Solomon?
- How could I "walk in the ways" of God today?

4

Week Four: God Judges Unfaithfulness to Covenant

As God's story continues do not let the details of the narrative overwhelm you. Keep *Reading* the story of God's activity in Scripture. Your small group is a place to *Discuss* how God is working in your life. The Echoes of God activity forces you to *Practice* listening for God's work in other's lives. As you *Reflect* on Scripture more and more associations may be made with your own journey of faith.

Day 1

▶ READ

Sometimes life in the story of God sucks. When the doctor says, "We did all we could do," or the banker says, "The grace period is up," or the father says, "I don't want it," we are shaken. Hope fails when promises are stamped undeliverable. God seems "out of business" or he forecloses on our eager expectations. The faith we have vaporizes, or the faith we lack shrivels our soul. When life sucks, how do we see God in the story of life?

The Bible is God's story. God plays lead role, as one who creates, covenants, delivers, and leads people. The human role in the story is faithlessness and ingratitude. Humans cycle in and out of relationship with God when it is convenient. When God is faithful, humans are unfaithful. Let's explore stories that might share similar plot lines with our times of frustration and faithlessness.

When we last left Israel, the monarchy was in full power. Three kings brought God-anointed leadership and world dominance to the nation of Israel. However, maintaining a united state is difficult. David challenges his son, Solomon, to remember the covenant and follow the Law of Moses (1 Kings 2:2-4). His son seems up to the challenge. He builds a grand temple for God yet states that God prefers to dwell in thick darkness (1 Kings 8:12-13). Solomon, with his hands spread up in prayer, says this at the temple's dedication: "O, Lord God of Israel, there is no God like you in heaven above or on earth beneath, keeping covenant and steadfast love for your servants who walk before you with all their heart" (v. 22-23). Solomon's prayer is the one we pray together each week. It summarizes God's magnificence and our call to live faithfully before him. Solomon promises to walk before God faithfully and asks God to keep the promise to maintain an heir of David as king (v. 25). Solomon insightfully mentions that God dwelling on earth is far-fetched, because "heaven and earth cannot contain Yahweh" much less this temple. Solomon is up to the challenge of faithfulness.

But similar to our lives these are stories of tragedy. Despite praying inspiring words, Solomon turns to other gods. According to Scripture, the monarchy is lost due to human unfaithfulness. In time, God's people lose the monarchy, the promised land, Jerusalem, and the temple of God.

The first of three tragedies occurs at Solomon's death. The nation of twelve original tribes is split, creating two separate kingdoms. The ten tribes of the Northern Kingdom, Israel, rebel against Solomon's heir, Jeroboam, who is appointed king of the new nation. God's people are no longer one united people of God. These Northern tribes do not have one single godly king. No one pursues Yahweh. All the kings are evil.

Solomon's son, Rehoboam, leads the Southern Kingdom of Judah. The capital of Judah remains in Jerusalem. The kings leading the two tribes of the Southern Kingdom are godlier than the Northern, yet there are few who serve Yahweh. Imagine the kingdom split in twin towers: Israel in the North and Judah in the South.

The second tragedy relates to how God's people lose the promises and are close to being eliminated as a nation. This second tragedy is the first of twin towers that collapse on God's people. In the eighth-century BC, Assyria is the dominant world power. Assyrian armies come across the desert and destroy the Northern Kingdom of Israel in 722 BC. This defeat deals a blow to God's people. Scripture interprets this defeat as a direct result of rejection and sin against God (2 Kings 17:7-8, 12-15). God judges the Northern Kingdom of Israel unfaithful to his covenant, using a foreign nation. Life as God's people is not meant for *privilege* but as *obligation* for a certain way of living. We are chosen by God. There are lifestyle expectations, if we choose to live within the reign of his kingdom. Israel takes pride in being the people of God, but they fail to live as the people of God. So, God uses Assyria to discipline his people.

The third tragedy devastates the identity of God's people. Their identity is tied to the land, nation, and temple. Manasseh is an evil king, who does things detestable to Yahweh. He sacrifices his son, practices sorcery, and places an idol (an Asherah pole) in the temple of Yahweh. The idol and altar stand rival God. However, Jews expect Jerusalem to stand forever, because God said so. Manasseh clings to God's promise to David that God's name will dwell on the Jerusalem temple forever (2 Kings 21:7–8).

Manasseh is the worst king of Judah, yet his grandson is probably the greatest king. Josiah takes the throne at 8 years old. His extensive national reform begins with temple repair. In the renovations, the book of the Law of Moses is discovered. Most likely the book found is all or part of Deuteronomy. Josiah is the only king in the Bible to have the distinction of being called one who followed the Lord God with all of his heart, soul and strength (2 Kings 23:25), like Moses directed in Deuteronomy 6:4–5.

Josiah's reforms are not enough to save the nation from destruction. Within two hundred years after the North topples, the South tower falls in 587 BC. The world power Babylonians capture the Southern Kingdom of Judah and destroy the city of Jerusalem, ripping the temple of Yahweh apart. The final chapter of the volumes of Kings tells of the tragedy (2 Kgs 25:9–12; cf. 2 Chr 36; Jer 52). Not only are loved ones killed and homes destroyed but their identity as God's people is uprooted. Their place of privilege is left in shambles, and their faith in God is a smoldering ruin.

The division, decline, and destruction of the monarchy do not mean God rejects his people entirely. God still has promises to keep. When God makes promises, he keeps them. God does not break promises. Even though God's people lose national prominence and are captured and exiled, God still leads his people. All during this time of decline, the prophets voice God's leadership. The prophets function throughout the history of the Hebrew people as a spokesperson or mouthpiece for God. A prophet is a messenger who brings a contemporary message to God's people and sometimes to foreign people. The prophets receive these messages from God through an external or internal voice of God. Other times they see visions or dream dreams. In all cases, prophets are able to discern spiritual realities in contemporary circumstances and speak an accurate word from God into that situation. The prophets serve as "conscience" for the nation of God[1] and worship Yahweh. At times they speak against the spirit of the age, popular opinion, or political power.

The prophets often bear the consequences of their prophecies through punishment, abuse, rejection, and death. The rejection of prophets reveals that to be God's people often means bearing the consequence of the world's sins. To be God's man or woman is not to live in comfortable isolation but to be involved in the affairs of the world and experience the suffering that comes from those who reject God.

Four characteristics are typical of prophets. First, prophets are normally from among the people of Israel. They are not foreigners (Deut 18:15). Second, a prophet often anoints the king. Samuel anoints Kings Saul and David. Other times prophets condemn the sitting human king. Prophets always assert Yahweh as the real king.

The third attribute and the one that most people focus on is their "foretelling" the future. When used today, the word "prophet" often means one who can predict the future or see unknowable things of life in a crystal ball. This definition is not the primary one in Scripture. Prophets do not sit in booths predicting events. In this era, no more than five to ten percent of prophecy is predictive of the future.[2] Instead, prophecy has contemporary significance. That leads into the fourth attribute of a prophet and the most significant. Prophets are "forth" tellers. They speak forth in the name of the Lord God.

The final determining factor about prophecy is the truthfulness of the word from God (Deut 18:20–22). If prophecy comes true, then the prophet is legitimate. That is why some prophets who are the harshest critics of the kings and nations later are the most revered, leaving behind influential writings. This idea of "forth" telling is best explained in the Hebrew word for "prophet," *nabi*, which means "one who announces" or "one who is called." Prophets are called by God to announce the words of God.

From a practical standpoint, the prophets appear in different ways in the Bible. Some prophets are named and have their stories told like Nathan, Ahijah, Jehu, Elijah, Micaiah, and Elisha. These are mentioned in the Bible, but they do not leave behind writings. Other prophets

---

1. Newbigin, *A Walk Through the Bible*, 27.
2. Fee and Stuart, *How to Read the Bible for all it is Worth*, 166.

appear as authors. The Bible's table of contents lists the prophets by book size. The prophets are not listed in chronological order like the first books of the Old Testament. There are Major Prophets and Minor Prophets. Being "Major" or "Minor" has nothing to do with influence or popularity but with book length. The Major Prophetic books are Isaiah, Jeremiah, Ezekiel, Lamentations (attributed to Jeremiah), and Daniel. The twelve Minor prophetic books stretch from Hosea to Malachi.

Typically, a prophet gives messages around one of four themes. Sometimes prophets direct attention to the covenant, reminding people of God's promises and their obligations from the Law of Moses. Second, a prophet may bring a judgment message to indict people for not following God's will. A third type of message promises redemption. God redeems or justifies his people from some evil. Similarly, the fourth type of speech is future restoration. These messages of hope promise God's restoring relationship with the people. The prophets' messages are often communicated in creative metaphorical ways. For example, in Isaiah 5, God is the owner of a vineyard who expects a harvest of grapes but gets a bunch of wild, worthless grapes. One famous image portrays God as a potter in Jeremiah 18. God molds people into useful vessels. God's people can be workable or resistant. Another common image is of God as the shepherd who feeds, gathers, carries, and leads his people or sheep (Isaiah 40). These prophetic metaphors communicate God's message.

Here are two sample stories of two prophets. One prophet is from the north, and one is from the south. One prophet writes a large book and another, a small book. First, Hosea is prophet for the Northern Kingdom of Israel. Hosea's life is an acted parable. God has him marry a prostitute. While that is the major storyline, there is a story from Hosea about parents and children. Israel plays the part of a child that God raises (Hosea 11:1–5). God loves Israel like a child. Imagine God picking up this child and pinching his cheeks. God feeds him. God protects him. One day while shopping God calls out to Israel, but Israel runs away. Kids often sprint off from their parents. Usually, they are laughing. Kids love being chased. They love having their parent's attention. But Israel keeps on running and has no intention of being caught. So, God lets Israel go. Israel runs from God into the arms of Egyptian slavery. When we reject God, we also run to slavery and embrace chaos, disorder, and accept a self-ordered world.

Week Four: God Judges Unfaithfulness to Covenant   37

The second story is from Ezekiel. This graphic story easily is rated "R." In fact, the Bible contains many passages best classified as adult material. Ezekiel is one of those books. Ezekiel 16 contains an intriguing love story. This time Israel is a child born of two different parents in a foreign land. Cute little baby Israel has nothing more than her umbilical cord cut. She is left exposed out in the elements to die as an ancient abortion. No one cares. God happens to be strolling by the field and sees this newborn baby girl flopping around in her blood. God takes the unwanted baby as his own. She grows up into a full-figured girl, an eye-catching woman with curves in all the right places. When the young beautiful Israel is of an age to marry, God marries her. God enters into covenant wedlock with this beautiful princess. He gives her everything a princess could want: the most beautiful clothing, the most expensive perfumes, luxurious spa treatment, priceless jewelry, and even a queen's crown. Queen Israel does not even have to cook as a kitchen staff provides all her meals. This woman is absolutely gorgeous. She is like an Internet icon the world recognizes by face.

Israel gets bored and becomes a prostitute, selling her body to paying customers. She strips off all the beautiful clothing and jewels to please other men. The children she bears from these escapades are sacrificed to foreign gods and eaten. This story graphically describes rejection of God. She completely rejects God and his mercy.

Life in God's story sometimes sucks. We need prophets, who come into our lives and break into our self-absorbed stories. Prophets help us see that our story—our life—is not the only one that matters. You have control over your life, but you are part of something much bigger. You can participate in a significant story of God. Prophets help us become self-aware that what I do, and what happens to me, might be a divine classroom. Sometimes we are judged by God like these nations. Other times, we are like Josiah, rewarded by God. Sometimes we suffer for doing good like Jeremiah. In all cases, God instructs willing learners. We recognize our story has consequences. Those who trust God affirm that history may be interpreted in light of our relationship with God. Our personal morality affects us and those around us.

These stories have amazing endings. God delights in taking the wrecked, screwed-up messes we make of our lives and restoring them by his grace. He does it every time, if we surrender to him. When a doctor says, "We did all we could," God says, "I'm not finished." When the creditor ends the grace period, God's grace period has only begun. When the father says of the child, "I don't want it," God says, "I want you, I have always wanted you, and I always will." At the end of Hosea 11, with children running away, God roars like a lion and his children freeze in their tracks. They come back from all over the earth. Listen to the end of Ezekiel 16:59–60: "I will deal with you as you have done, you who have despised the oath, breaking the covenant; yet I will remember my covenant with you in the days of your youth, and I will establish you with an everlasting covenant." God is faithful through our unfaithfulness so that we will be "confounded and never open [our] mouths again because of [our] shame, when [God] forgives everything" (16:63). This story of God is absolutely breathtaking. God is faithful in punishment, which is for the purpose of restoration.

Day 2

▷▶ DISCUSS

Small Group Discussion (60 minutes)

The small group gathering is a time to listen and share stories. Our lives are sacred spaces where God is working. Listen for the echoes of God's work in each one of the group members.

Move 1: Sharing Prayer Conversation (15 minutes)

- For what are you *thankful*?
- How have you *seen God at work*?
- For what are you *sorry*?
- To whom do you *need to show love*?

Move 2: Listening to Others' Stories (30 minutes)

- Tell an experience of a "guaranteed for life" product you bought that did not last.
- Think about a time when your normal routine was affected by a change (without electricity or a car was in the shop or money was

> **Leader:**
> By this week, the sharing ritual may become a comfortable space for group sharing. Openness develops among people willing to share their lives with others.

tight). Consider how your expectations of normal compare with what others in the group (or world) might list.

- Talk about how the "echoes of God" activities are affecting your perception of other people.

MOVE 3: *TELLING* STORIES (10 MINUTES)

- The Listening Leader articulates connections between the stories told in the session and the story of God from the reading of Scripture.
- For example, compare the broken product stories shared by the group with how Israel broke covenant with God or point out ways we expect God is always on our side.

> **LEADER:**
> You have spent the group time listening and helping others listen. Now, make connections with God's story based on what you heard.

MOVE 4: *CONNECTING* CONVERSATION PRAYER (5 MINUTES)

> **LEADER:**
> Before dismissing the group, describe the Echoes of God activity. Feel free to adjust it or use a different practice. Encourage group members to practice listening for God's echoes this week.

- This prayer time begins by reciting 1 Kings 8:23 together:

O Lord, God of Israel, there is no God like you
in heaven above or on earth beneath,
keeping covenant and steadfast love
for your servants who walk before you with all
their heart.

- Leader ends with a prayer that reflects some of the stories and conversations from the group discussion.

DAYS 3—7

▷▷▶ PRACTICE

Echoes of God Activity

While at work or at home (or even online), listen for stories that communicate hope and hopelessness. Bring a list of these episodes next week. Determine whether your heart is inclined toward hope or hopelessness. Journal about what you discover.

▷▷▷▶ REFLECT

The Story & My Story

These Scripture readings and questions are for reflection. Question one reflects on the text and the second on "My Story." If you have less time read only the underlined chapter.

Day 3: 1 Kings <u>8</u>, 11–13

- Notice and list all the things God does in this section.
- What areas of my life do I keep God from ruling?

> **Reminder:**
>
> Each day this week listen for Echoes of God in stories you hear about hope or hopelessness. You can share them at the next group session.

Day 4: 2 Kings 1–<u>4</u>

- What does it mean to be a "man (person) of God?"
- What physical circumstances are hindering my trust in God?

Day 5: 2 Chronicles 33, <u>34</u>–36

- When is God moved to action?
- What do I need to "rediscover" in my relationship with God?

Day 6: Hosea 1–5, <u>11</u>

- In what ways does Israel act like a rebellious child?
- In what situations do I pout, sass, or run away from God?

Day 7: Ezekiel 8–11, <u>16</u>

- What is amazing about how God acts as a husband in this story?
- How would I treat my spouse if he/she acted like the one in the story?

5

Week Five: God Remains Faithful

Last week in the story of God we were left in a state of hopelessness with God's people. However, this week God shows his faithfulness in spite of human unfaithfulness. Take time to *Read* over the material before your small group meets to *Discuss*.

DAY 1

▶ READ

What will life in America look like when it falls? Using the word "when" is intentional. No world power has ever lasted forever. There is no promise from God that America will last forever. Americans wrongly assume and believe that there will be no end to prosperity but things change. Look at shopping centers. A new shopping area is erected in a new part of town, but within a few decades it is run down and on the wrong side of town. When your world collapses, things change. When imprisoned by the darkness of trouble, life is different. Thomas Pettepiece tells the story of his political imprisonment as a Christian. There were no Bibles available. There was no bread or wine for communion. Secretly the believers gathered and broke imaginary bread saying, "This is the body of Christ given for you." They drank imaginary wine and whispered, "This is the blood of Christ given for you." The non-believing prisoners agreed to provide noise interference so the Christians could worship. When the non-Christians observed their practice of faith, they were moved. One remarked that for the first time they saw what faith looked like.[1]

---

1. Job and Shawchuck, *A Guide to Prayer*, 143–144.

In the last chapter, the story of God is done. God's Kingdom divides, declines, and is destroyed. It ends like a movie you know will end in tragedy. You exit the theatre shuffling along with lead in your shoes and despair on your shoulders. God blesses the city of David, which is a ransacked ash heap. The temple is a smoldering ruin, and the tall wall is gravel. There seems to be no hope and no God in the world.

The historical dates 722 and 587 BC are national burial markers of a dead religion. In 722 BC, Assyrian powers destroy the larger Northern Kingdom of Israel. Maybe God will take care of the smaller kingdom centered on the dynasty of David, temple worship, and the capital of Jerusalem. The surviving little nation of Judah thinks it will last forever. Two hundred years later the new world power of Babylon destroys Jerusalem and the temple of Yahweh in 587 BC. King Hezekiah sees his nation and faith destroyed, his sons are executed, and then his eyes are gouged out for a long walk into Babylonian captivity. King Hezekiah's name means "Yahweh strengthens." Hezekiah is a portrait of the blind hope of God's people.

The Northern tribes of Israel are carted off into Assyrian captivity, and then the Southern tribes are exiled to Babylonian cities. God's people are removed from their homes. These foreign captors take the best people, the royalty like Daniel or later Esther, and relocate them, scattering them across the known world. The poor and ignorant are left behind. Many of God's people no longer care about Yahweh or his foreclosed promises to Abraham. They move on with their lives. They find new gods and new customs. Foreign life strips away the old faith. God's people are never the same. Babylonian oppression gives way to Persian mercy. Then, Alexander the Great takes over the world, and Greek culture dominates the Middle East from 333–31 BC. Later, the Romans dominate. Throughout history God's people trade one tyrant for another.

During the Babylonian captivity, which lasts about seventy years, some continue to think about Yahweh and cry. Psalm 137 is a graphic lament. God's people sit by the rivers of Babylon and sob. They hang their musical instruments in the willow trees and weep. The Babylonians in jest or ridicule say, "Sing us one of those Zion victory songs." But God's people refuse to sing songs of victory while they are prisoners in a foreign land. Instead, they promise never to forget Jerusalem and to destroy their oppressors. They never will forget their entire city being stripped to the foundations like an F-8 tornado, while the Babylonians cheer. God's people think, "If we were in God's shoes, we would have rejected us, too; but God could start over." However, the God who uses powerful foreign kings to teach judgment also uses foreign kings to restore worship of the one true and living God. The hero of the story is God and not Israel, Judah, or us. God refuses to permit his story—the story of God—to drown in tears of failure.

The story must be reevaluated and reinterpreted. If God can allow the destruction of his people and his temple, then something has been missed. There is more to this story than holy places. The Bible's table of contents reveals that from Genesis to Esther the story is told basically in chronological order. The books in exception are Ruth and Esther, which tell the story of two women in detail, and the Chronicles which re-tell the Kings stories. The books First Kings and Second Kings are negative portrayals of why the countries unravel and are destroyed. The Chronicles retell the same historical story, but from a new more positive perspective after the exile. The bumps of the kings are smoothed with hope in Chronicles. David is portrayed more positively, reducing the whole "Bathsheba" incident by not mentioning her name.

The Chronicles provide a new angle on the fall of the kingdom and express theological hope in "the remnant." The prophets often speak about a "remnant" of the people, which literally means "tent peg." Imagine a tent pitched in the desert. A huge tornado-like wind rips the tent up and throws it far away. All that remains of the tent site is a tent peg—a remnant. Prophets claimed God will rebuild his nation back from this one tent peg. Picture a house destroyed by a tornado. From one pipe sticking up from the ground an entire city is built.

Another important Hebrew word is *hesed*. It means "steadfast love" and points to how God's love endures and abides. God's love endures through creating, entering covenant with Abraham, delivering through Moses, pointing to covenant with the law, and in good and bad times. *Hesed* describes the constant loyalty of God. The theme verse (1 Kings 8:23) relates that God's love is steadfast. At a deep level trust in God's *hesed* is trust that God reigns despite contrary circumstances.

Hope is born when Babylon loses its power to Persia. In 538, King Cyrus of Persia, issues an edict, cleverly recorded as "the Edict of Cyrus" (2 Chronicles 36:22–23; cf. Ezra 1:1–4). Cyrus' decree amazingly recognizes Yahweh, God of heaven as the source of his power. Unbelievably this foreign king sends God's people home in his first year. God moves Cyrus to rebuild the temple of Yahweh. Cyrus is called God's anointed (Isaiah 45:1, 4, 13). What happened to David and the lineage of David? God chooses and uses foreigners to establish his kingdom, instill hope, and bless others. This edict from Cyrus fulfills the rejected and abused prophet Jeremiah's prophecy (25:11-12; 29:10).

After seventy years, the people travel back home. What is different after this 300-year exile experience? There are four results of the captivity. First, the wickedness of Israel is punished. Within history, God's people suffer as a result of corporate sin and rejection of God. Second, idolatry ends. Specifically, worship of many gods is condemned. Many Jews begin worshiping foreign gods. So, the change is short-lived. Third, the word of God (*Torah*) receives a new emphasis. With the priestly and sacrificial system destroyed along with the temple, a new approach to faith is needed. Prison changes the practice of faith. Rituals are replaced with "the book." Scribes replace priests. The word is a treasure to be preserved. Fourth, a new location for worship emerges. The synagogue replaces the temple. During the exile, Jews gathered to learn the stories. They became a "people of the book," learning the Torah. Eventually, this learning produces expert scribes, Sadducees, and the Pharisees, who are the best example of rigorously following of the Law of Moses.

Now, here are three stories about a king, a scribe, and a politician who return God's people to the land. Scholars debate these three return trips, but most of the controversy is about whether or not Ezra and Nehemiah were contemporaries. These debates are acknowledged but not entered here. The three trips are taken in the order they appear in the Bible.

King Zerubbabel leads the first return (538–515 BC). He is the grandson of Johoiakim, great grandson of Josiah, and the best of Judah's kings. While Zerubbabel has royal lineage, his name means "offspring of Babylon." Zerubbabel is mentioned in Jesus' genealogy in Matthew 1. As the grandson of a king born into exile, he knows nothing but exile. Leading the return, he first restores the altar of God (Ezra 3:2-3). Worship comes first. When most countries rebuild a nation (i.e. Iraq) they build the army, establish law, and then build churches, synagogues, or mosques. However, worship of Yahweh was priority. In Ezra 3:10-13, the foundation for the temple is laid first in thanks to God "for he is good, for his steadfast love endures forever toward Israel."

The people need some prophetic prompting to build the Lord's house. The people are slow and require a reminder message from the prophet Haggai. It takes Persian kings to move them. The foreign Persian kings Cyrus and Artaxerxes are part of the restoration of Israel's religion. This time it is King Darius who issues a decree to remind them of the earlier Edict of Cyrus. Haggai explains that they need first to build God's house and then God will bless the building of their houses. The "remnant" people hear Haggai and obey the word of the Lord (Haggai 1:12-14).

The second trip back is led by Ezra (458-456 BC), who is a teacher and scribe well-trained in the Law of Moses (Ezra 7:6). About fifty-seven years after the restoration of the altar and temple, Ezra returns people to the covenant (Ezra 7:9-10). Ezra's heart is on the study, practice, and teaching of the law. He believes, practices, and teaches it.

Ezra falls to his knees, spreads his hands to the sky, and repents for the wickedness of the nation (Ezra 9:5-9). Ezra thanks God for paying attention to a small remnant of people, to give them a stake in the future. He thanks God for his steadfast love that they can rebuild the holy place and build a wall because of the merciful kings of Persia.

In Nehemiah 8-10, Ezra climbs up to a special wooden platform, where all can hear him. He reads the law from early in the morning until mid-day to a mixed crowd of men and women and older children. As Ezra explains it plainly to them, they weep in sorrow for how they have lived in rejection of God. For weeks he teaches them. Finally, everyone dresses up in funeral clothes to sign an agreement to keep the law of God.

The third return is led by Nehemiah about twelve years later (444-432 BC). Nehemiah, a high-ranking and trusted official, is cup bearer to the king of Persia. He taste-tests the king's food. When he hears the condition of his homeland and Jerusalem, Nehemiah spends days weeping, praying, and fasting (Neh 1:4-9). When he goes to serve the king wine, Nehemiah is still terribly sad. The king knows him well and notices his sadness of heart. The king asks how he can help Nehemiah. Silently Nehemiah prays to God and then asks to be sent on a mission to rebuild the city of Jerusalem. The king agrees. Nehemiah asks the king for protection letters and for free lumber. The king complies with every request. Nehemiah leaves Susa in Persia and goes to his homeland as a politician to rebuild the wall around the famous city of Jerusalem.

God uses Zerubbabel, Ezra, and Nehemiah—a king, a scribe, and a politician—to reverse Israel's fortunes, restoring them to the land. More amazing is the fact that God also uses pagan foreign kings—Cyrus, Darius, and Artexerxes—to express his steadfast love and keep his promises going.

During this time, the prophets still call people to repentance. There is a love story in the final book in the Old Testament. Malachi's love story is a fit closing to this chapter. The prophet Malachi's message was simple, "You have despised and rejected God," and God is not pleased with faithlessness. Malachi spells out how they reject God, but the people play dumb and question him. The book begins by affirming God's love in the midst of the rubble of destruction and the pain of exile. But, the people question God's love saying, "How have you loved us?" (Malachi 1:2). When Malachi says the people have failed to honor God, they retort, "How?" (1:6). Malachi says they have wearied the Lord by turning away from the law (2:17). The point is they must return to God, and he will return to them. God does not change but invites us to change our rebellious ways and seek Him. While some question God's love, one of the funniest things God can say is basically: "The best proof that I love you is that you are not dead yet" (3:6).

So what about us? When we try to rebuild our lives, we start with wanting God to provide a wall of protection. Then, we will follow the rules. Finally, we might worship. But this is not the story we should live. When hope is gone and comfort is removed, we trust the steadfast love of God to show love to a faithful remnant of people. When life gives reason to doubt, we first lift up God as king in worship. We bow our lives to God's guidance through story. We let God be our wall of protection.

Day 2

▷▶ DISCUSS

Small Group Discussion (60 minutes)

The small group time is enhanced when group members *Read* prior to the group gathering as background for *Discussion*. The overall experience is improved as the group *Practices* Echoes of God activity and the *Reflect* readings and questions. Setting aside a few minutes each day makes the process transformative.

Move 1: *Sharing* Prayer Conversation (15 minutes)

- For what are you *thankful*?
- How have you *seen God at work*?
- For what are you *sorry*?
- To whom do you *need to show love*?

Move 2: *Listening* to Others' Stories (30 minutes)

- Describe a time when you felt exiled from God.
- Tell about a time in your life when you were shown love and you did not deserve that love.
- Share a conversation or story about hope (or hopelessness) from the past week of doing the "echoes of God" activity.

Move 3: *Telling* Stories (10 minutes)

- The Listening Leader articulates connections among the stories told in the session and the story of God from the reading or Scripture.
- For example, a leader might connect the group's stories of hopelessness with the story of the God who does not forget us but brings hope to our hopeless situations.

> **Leader:**
> This week you may invite a group member to make a connection between 'The Story' and the stories people shared.

Move 4: *Connecting* Conversation Prayer (5 minutes)

- This prayer time begins by reciting 1 Kings 8:23 together:

> **Leader:**
> Before the group dismisses, describe one of the Echoes of God activities. Challenge group members to practice one this week.

*O Lord, God of Israel,
there is no God like you
in heaven above or on earth beneath,
keeping covenant and steadfast love
for your servants who walk before you
with all their heart.*

- Leader ends with a prayer that reflects some of the stories and conversations from the group discussion.

Days 3—7

▷▷▶ PRACTICE

Echoes of God Activity

Activity 1: Security may be found through religious, physical, or legal means. How do laws, religious groups, and security systems provide limited security in life?

or

Activity 2: Read the newspaper or online magazine. Look for stories tied to people's fear of losing religious, political, or national power.

▷▷▷▶ REFLECT

The Story & My Story

These Scripture readings and questions are for reflection. The first question reflects on the text, and the second reflects on "My Story." If you have less time read only the underlined chapter.

Day 3: Isaiah 6, 8–<u>10</u>

- What is the purpose of God's anger?
- How has God's judgment affected me personally?

Day 4: Daniel <u>1</u>–3

- How does Daniel seek the ways of God in his life?
- In what areas of life is my faithfulness to God being challenged?

> **Reminder:**
> Each day is an opportunity to do one of the Echoes activities about security. You might use a sticky-note to put a reminder on a mirror or car dashboard.

Day 5: Ezra <u>1</u>, 3–5

- How does God use all people for his purposes (Jews and foreigners)?
- How has God taught me something through the life of a non-Christian (or someone different from me)?

Day 6: Nehemiah 1, 2–4

- How does Nehemiah show his dependence upon God?
- When am I inclined to pray?

Day 7: Malachi 1, 2–4

- In what ways have God's people despised and rejected God?
- What is God "tired of" in my life?

6

Week Six: God's People Respond in Worship and Wisdom

The first testament or Old Testament concludes this week. This week explores the human response to God's faithfulness as worship and wise living. This week as you *Read, Discuss, Practice,* and *Reflect,* consider how your life responds to God's action.

DAY 1

▶ READ

The silent movie glows in black on white. Live piano music provides the background drama and emotion to fill the void of words. A curly blonde's eyes are saucers. Cotton ropes hold her to the steel tracks as she is about to be iron-pressed by a steam engine. In rides the hero, who cuts the ropes and saves the day. Does this sound cliché?

The story of the Bible has one hero: God. The heroine played by humans is cute but leaves much to be desired. Humans often follow heroes other than God. How does one respond to God's rescue? Some respond in committed love. Others react in fear. Some seem to know God is their rescuer, and others wonder if God has bound them to the track of death. The question is this: "How do we respond to God?"

The storyline of the Old Testament is complete. The people of God have been rescued, but they are no longer a dominant force in the world. They are a captive people. How will they respond to their creator who has delivered them again? One Psalmist asks and answers this question in Psalm 116:12-13. Imagine a man comes into the temple. He personally experienced God saving him from destruction, perhaps in a battle for his life or homeland. After God's deliverance, the man responds by toasting God's salvation. He raises a glass of wine and calls on the name of God. The raising of the glass is a commitment in everyone's sight to pay vows to God. This story portrays a man worshiping God with a toast and vowing to live faithful to God. These are two fitting responses to God's deliverance. One is worship living and one is wisdom living. The primary divine act of God's love prompts a secondary response of loving God. 1 John 4:19, we love because God first loves us. Our story is simple: God loves, so we love.

Another example of human response is the two tablets given to Moses. These ten commands identify God (Exodus 20:2-6; Deuteronomy 5:6-10) and remind us of God's star power. The hero is the "I Am," the God who always is, was, and will be. This God delivers us. The Ten Commandments call us to worship this one God only. Then, the commands point us to live the life into which God calls us. Worship comes first, and ethics come second. Hearts break out in praise. Hands stretch out in action. These two responses—worship and wisdom—shape the story of human response.

There is a grouping of literature in the Old Testament called the "Wisdom Literature." Wisdom is contained in the repeated refrain "the fear of the Lord," which guides wisdom. These books are Proverbs, Ecclesiastes, and Job. Sometimes Psalms and Song of Solomon are placed in the wisdom or poetic literature, but they will be dealt with in "worship." Wisdom refers both to these books loaded with wisdom and also to a way of thinking. Some might call wisdom a theology, philosophy, or paradigm of thought.

One of Israel's treasured possessions is the wisdom refrain, "the fear of the Lord is the beginning of wisdom." This phrase, the "fear of God," is an underground chamber loaded with jewels of meaning. The wisdom literature is full of references to the fear of Yahweh. However, at times Scripture encourages us to "fear God" and other times God says, "Do not fear" or "Do not be afraid." So which is it: do not fear God or fear God?

Here are some rapid fire clips from God's story about "fear." Abraham shows "fear of Yahweh" when he obeys by almost sacrificing his son (Genesis 22:12). Some people and places are described as having "no fear of God" (Genesis 20:11). "The fear" is even a code name for God. Isaac's God, Yahweh, is called "the fear" (Genesis 31:42). Abram falls on his face in one of many encounters with God (17:3). A shoeless

Moses bows before the bush burning with God's presence. God identifies himself as the God of Abraham, Isaac, and Jacob. Moses hides his face in terror (Exodus 3:6) even before he hears the secret name of God: Yahweh. The people of God, newly freed from Egyptian slavery, tremble in fear at the foot of Mount Sinai observing a smoking mountain with lightening flashing and thunder booming (Exodus 19:16). After Moses gets the Ten Commandments, the people beg him not to let God speak to them again (Exodus 20:18–21). There is a difference between the fear God's presence creates and the requirement to fear God. When God shows up, people are afraid because God is extremely holy and we are not. When God's leaders speak, they call people to live in the fear of the Lord. Still, how do we fear God?

The fear of Yahweh is not emotional anxiety. People are not asked to live in a state of apprehension of God. The *practice of fearing God* is a human response that offers loyalty to God. People give God the honor that God deserves. This response is worship. We lift the name of God in praise, and we remind ourselves of the requirement of loyalty. God does not need our praise, but we live our stories in a way that shows loyalty to God. Worship is a consciousness-forming experience. In fact, when people enter the presence of God, they cannot escape worship. Worship happens naturally. Worship is our preliminary response to God. We cannot help but worship God.

Fear of God has a second meaning that is ethical. Those who fear God turn from evil and all things that oppose God. They no longer live in the stories of hate, evil, anger, and discord. In this way, fear of Yahweh is the beginning of wisdom or of living wisely. Wisdom is deeper than knowledge. Wisdom is practical knowledge of life. Wisdom is the art of living well. Someone may have knowledge evidenced by many degrees yet not be wise. The reverse is true. Someone may be wise yet not have factual knowledge or any academic degree. Wisdom and knowledge are connected but different.

Humans respond to God's mercy through worship. The word "worship" often is associated with corporate, gathered worship. Worship is an event to praise God. However, worship is also when a community recognizes God's work in their experiences. The weekly repetition of worship is so important because what people repeatedly do together forms them. Prayer, Scripture, preaching, Lord's Supper, singing, giving, witnessing, and other elements shape our lives. In worship, we participate in a story that glorifies God. After years of worship our human story unites with God's story. Worship trains hearts to focus on God rather than hate, violence, revenge, or self. Worship acknowledges we are not God.

Three worship books tell the story of our human response to God. First is the Psalms, a collection of songs unique to all of Scripture. The Psalms express our words to God. Have you considered that these words are authoritative Scripture, but they do not come from God? They are offered to God, and they are worship. The Psalms describe human passion as praise, thanksgiving, pleading, wisdom, anger, fear, depression, sadness, lament, and so much more. They honestly reflect real life as worship to God. The Psalms show that *there is space for wide-ranging emotion in responding to God.* The five collections or books of the 150 Psalms form Israel's hymnbook and prayer book. The Psalms are people's speech to God in humanity, honesty, and hope. They are a human voice to God. They declare hope in God for salvation. God's story is told using our words to God. The diverse life experiences and stories in Psalms are offered to God in a way similar to how this small group experience offers life to God.

A second worship book is the greatest song, the sex song, the Song of Solomon. The Bible contains a whole book devoted to sex. This epic song *makes space for joy.* Within this lyrical love poem, sexual freedom within marriage is celebrated. In our age of sexual confusion, sex is praised within marriage. Sometimes Christian people make this a symbolic poem about God as the groom and God's people the bride. Sex is a valuable, God created part of life that is to be celebrated. Sex reveals the intimate relationship humans may have with God. This song is proof that life is worship before God. As Paul writes, our worship presents our bodies as living sacrifices holy and pleasing to God (Romans 12:1-2). The human body is not presented to the world's sexual patterns. What a blessing that the Bible contains a story of sexuality as an example of worship!

Lamentations, the final book of worship, is most often placed in the major prophetic books. However, the Lamentations contain five lament songs of the country of Judah while in Babylonian captivity. These poems express tremendous sorrow. Attributed to Jeremiah, the weeping prophet, Lamentations show that worship *makes space for sorrow before God.* Worship needs time for sorrow. The sorrow can be a confessional sorrow for sin or sorrow for the condition of life. The tragedies of war, violence, suffering, poverty, hate, and crime may be brought into worship. God may be addressed on any and every occasion. Sorrow needs space in the church pew, or it will destroy lives from the inside out. Sorrow has a place in worship.

There are also three stories that tell the human response of wisdom. First, the book of Proverbs is a collection of truisms that reveal *the benefits of wisdom and consequences of foolishness*. Most people think of Proverbs as those short phrases that are clever and true. Rarely do preachers or churches teach the book of Proverbs, because it seems like a random coffee table book of sayings. We like them, even love them, but they seem too diverse to teach. However, Proverbs is a hidden story.

Imagine the setting of Proverbs: a father and son chat about sex. One of the more uncomfortable times in the life of a father is when he unpacks the mysteries of life to his son through the sex talk. All of life is described through sex, which grabs a young man's attention. This Dad explains life as a choice between the wisdom woman, who I call "Sophia" after the Greek word for wisdom, and folly, who I call "Paula" because it sounds like folly. Life is made of choices between good and evil, wisdom and foolishness. We want our children to learn to make good, wise choices and learn the way of wisdom. This path to wisdom begins in fear of Yahweh (Proverbs 1:7). When people respect there is a God, they live differently. We live in God's story. The Proverbs collection closes with the wisdom woman, the perfect wife. She does not deceive with flirting, sexy features but lives in fear and respect of God. The Bible contains a story about life's choices as a "proverbial" sex talk.

A second book, Ecclesiastes, shows *the futility of wisdom*. Imagine a wood-paneled room with professor Solomon leading a somewhat depressing philosophical and intellectual discourse on the meaning of life. This professor tries to find the meaning of life apart from God (read 1:12–14). His collection of poems, proverbs, and essays concludes that life is meaningless. In other words, even wisdom is a futile pursuit that increases sorrow and suffering. In the closing line of Ecclesiastes, the teacher provides readers with the sum duty of humankind: fear God and keep his commandments, because in the end all that is good and evil will be revealed in the brightness of God's truth (Ecclesiastes 12:13–14). The aim is loyal respect and worship of God. Our human stories can find encouragement in the fact that the Bible contains a story relating life's meaninglessness.

Finally, there is the famous story of Job, which teaches *the limits of wisdom*. Good cannot be locked up into eternal rules. Job's suffering bucks up against the prosperity gospel we all want to be true. We like to believe that doing good things means you get good things in return. We would love for "karma" to be the way of the world. The standardized wisdom thought is this: "You reap what you sow." In Deuteronomy 30:15–18, Moses sets before the people of God a choice between life and death. Life means obeying the commands, loving God, and walking in the ways of God. That is a good choice. Death is disobeying the commands and serving other gods: a bad choice. Job's friends were not much help. Eliphaz looks at Job—who has a dead family, no money, and terrible health issues—and uses the wisdom principle. You must have done something wrong. If you plow iniquity and sow trouble, then you reap the same (Job 4:6–8). This comment is not encouraging. In Job's story, the destruction of his prosperity, family, and health is not the result of his unrighteousness. The book of Job attacks the wisdom principle that if you do good you get good and if you do evil you get evil. God is not a behavioralist. He is not a vending machine where you can put a dollar into a machine, push "Cola," and get Cola. Sometimes in life you get grape. Job teaches that there are *limits to responding in wisdom*. At times we seek God in pain (Job 28:28). The true human story is well represented by the Bible's inclusion of a book that questions the suffering in life.

So, how will the damsel, no longer in distress, respond to God? God does not place humanity on the tracks. The tracks are the consequences of humans who play the hero themselves or trust other heroes. We respond to God in worship and wisdom. Worship expresses the entirety of life's emotion, joy, and sorrow to God. Wisdom is a lived expression of "fearing the Lord." But neither one is enough to save the world.

The prophet Isaiah cautions those who reduce their response to God to either worship or wisdom (Isaiah 29:13–14). Worship has become rote. We give lip worship to God but not heart worship. Our hearts worship Best Buy, Macy's, or the pool man. God will not accept empty worship tagged onto our consumptive, self-oriented lives. God will destroy worship that lacks wise living.

Our failure to worship God and live before him in wisdom sets the stage for the greatest event in the history of the world. In this Old Testament story, the seeds are sown for something new. From a dead stump of a nation, God is growing a man (Isaiah 11:1–3a). A man is coming who will have God's spirit and live in wisdom, fear of the Lord, and act in God's righteousness. The world will never be the same.

Day 2

▷▶ DISCUSS

Small Group Discussion (60 minutes)

This week marks the midpoint of the study, plus the group completes a survey of the Old Testament section of God's story. Hopefully the group has become comfortable and natural with sharing their life stories and exploring how those stories connect. God's pursuit of us continues with a look at how we respond to God's love.

Move 1: *Sharing* Prayer Conversation (15 minutes)

- For what are you *thankful*?
- How have you *seen God at work*?
- For what are you *sorry*?
- To whom do you *need to show love*?

> **Leader:**
> Congratulate the group on their open sharing and their work to *Read, Discuss, Practice,* and *Reflect* on God's story. Remind them that this process is more than the content, but it is about offering God the content of our lives.

Move 2: *Listening* to Others' Stories (30 minutes)

- Share some stories about security from the echoes of God activity last week.
- Describe a time when you were aware of (or in awe of) God.
- What are your everyday sources of wisdom (people, places, resources, etc.)?

Move 3: *Telling* Stories (10 minutes)

- The Listening Leader articulates connections between the stories told in the session and the story of God from the reading or Scripture.
- For example, the leader might express how the Sharing Prayer time is a worshipful response to God out of the good and bad in our lives. The stories participants share may show indications of our worshipful living before God.

Week Six: *God's People Respond in Worship and Wisdom*

MOVE 4: CONNECTING CONVERSATION PRAYER (5 MINUTES)

- This prayer time begins by reciting 1 Kings 8:23 together:

*O Lord, God of Israel, there is no God like you
in heaven above or on earth beneath,
keeping covenant and steadfast love
for your servants who walk before you with
all their heart.*

- Leader ends with a prayer that reflects some of the stories and conversations from the group discussion.

> **LEADER:**
> Before the group dismisses, describe the Echoes of God activity and challenge group members to practice echoing this week.

DAYS 3—7

▷▷▶ PRACTICE

Echoes of God Activity

Notice what people esteem (worship) by the priority they give it with their time, money, energy, etc. Who do people consider wise? In casual conversation, ask different people "who do you see as wise?"

▷▷▷▶ REFLECT

The Story & My Story

These Scripture readings and questions are for reflection. The first question reflects on the text and the second on "My Story." If you have less time read only the underlined chapter.

Day 3: Job 1–3, <u>28</u>, 42

- How is "wisdom" revealed in Job's life?
- Do I seek wisdom?

Day 4: Psalms <u>1</u>–5

- What is God's role in prayer?
- How do these ancient prayers speak to me today?

Day 5: Proverbs 1–5

- What are characteristics of the way of wisdom?
- When was a time that I chose the "path of wisdom?"

Day 6: Ecclesiastes 1–3, 11, 12

- What is the difference between wisdom and knowledge?
- What is the purpose of my life?

Day 7: Song of Solomon 1, 2–8

- How is faithfulness a wise choice?
- What is "true" love?

> **LEADER:**
>
> This week observe things people worship or value in everyday life. Consider whether those things are worth the time and money we invest in them.

7

Week Seven: God Lives Among His People

This week the story of God meets the story of humanity. In this stunning move from heaven to earth, God lives among humanity as Jesus Christ. The *Read, Discuss, Practice,* and *Reflect* sections of this week invite us to see God's story and the human story as joined together in Jesus.

DAY 1

▶ READ

The story of God is in progress. To stop with the Old Testament leaves the story finished, immobile. God's narrative is always in motion. God created a world but would not force humans to worship one God. God blessed people descending from Abraham but would not require them to live within the promise. God delivered Hebrews from slavery but that did not keep them from cursing their deliverer. God gave them the law, but its guidance did not make them holy. God provided leaders, judges, and kings, but they treated God as one among many other gods. God punished their rebellion, but some left God forever. God showed constant love to them and commitment to the promises made, but God did not force their love. The kingdom of God still is not recognized and Israel is a weak, captive people.

Some of the Israelites still believe God will establish his kingdom. But how can Yahweh save them? God's people have been defeated, deported, and sent back to devastated land. There is little hope. However, people cling to hope that the kingdom of God might be established in one of four ways.[1] First, a political revolt against foreign powers may

---

1. Newbigin, *A Walk Through the Bible*, 46–48.

establish the kingdom. They can rebel against oppressors, whether Assyrians, Babylonians, Persians, Greeks or Romans, and reorganize. Some think Israel is one coup away from a regime change to establish the kingdom of God. During the Greek occupation, the Macabees fight and lose. During Jesus' time, there are political zealots. A variety of Messiahs spring up as potential kings for Israel.

A second hope utilizes cooperation. Rather than violence, these are the voices of accommodation and compromise. The Sadducees take this stance. They are an old-school tradition of upper-class priests from the line of the Davidic priest, Zaddok. The priests who maintain the temple, sacrifices, and rituals often support Herodian rule. This cooperative approach works within the system to establish the kingdom of God.

A third hope spiritualizes the kingdom of God through keeping the Law of Moses. The kingdom is treated as merely something spiritual. People enter the kingdom by following spiritual laws. The Pharisees, whose name means "separate ones," embody this hope. They separate themselves through strict adherence to the law and do not assimilate foreign religion.

A fourth hope is withdrawal from the temple system into a monastic community. The desert community—known as the Essenes—rebels against the temple system. They leave Jerusalem with temple Scripture scrolls and go to the desert to form a new community at Qumran. Their language is similar in style to John's gospel and to John the Baptizer.

These four kingdom hopes do not exclude one another but overlap, especially in the hope for a king to restore rule. Jesus is hope revealed—the promised Messiah or king. "Messiah" is Hebrew, and "Christ" is Greek meaning king. Jeremiah prophesied (Jeremiah 23:5–6) that God was sending a son of David to reign as king and save Israel and Judah. He would be called "Yahweh is our Righteousness." Isaiah prophesied that a twig would grow from the dead stump of God's people and Yahweh, God's Spirit, would be on him (Isaiah 11:1–3). This is what people expect: a king from the line of David and in the power of Yahweh-God. The people want a king to make their political, religious, economic, and social dreams come true. However, Jesus explodes all expectations for Messiah.

The story of Jesus centers on his birth, life, death, and resurrection. Jesus is born the illegitimate son of Joseph and Mary, Nazarenes from the Galilee region of Israel. Jesus is everything a king is not. He is not royalty. He does not fight. He is controversial. Jesus takes the mantle of Messiah but avoids the label. He dies as a criminal. Every human is born, lives, and dies, yet Jesus redefines human life at each of these moments. Jesus' birth as the son of God by a virgin woman shows *God with us*. Jesus' life is an example of *God among us*. Jesus' death reveals *God suffering for us* and shows the way to life is through sacrificial death to self. The resurrection is *God living in spite of us*. This is gospel.

What is gospel? It is a slippery word, which Christians use like oxygen but rarely stop to define. Sometimes Christians say things like: "Believe the gospel," "Obey the gospel," "Proclaim the gospel," "The gospel truth," or "Worthy of the gospel." To this tiny word Christians hook railroad car after railroad car of data, meaning, and doctrine.

The word "gospel" means "good news" or "exciting message." Good news announces the birth of a child and victory over foes. The good news is only good news, if it meets the expectations of my perspective. Good news is Oklahoma beats Texas in college football. Good news is all terrorists are defeated. Certainly, good news depends upon your point of view. At its core, the good news is the story of God expressed in Jesus and not endless doctrine.

The gospel is also a "genre," a type of literature: the life story of God. The New Testament contains gospels, which describe the life of Jesus, specifically his baptism, ministry in Galilee, ministry in Jerusalem, and his passion or suffering death. In Luke's account the word "gospel" announces the good news of Jesus' birth (2:10), a sermon in Luke 4, actions to tell John the Baptist (7:22), and the content of preaching (8:1; 9:6; 16:16; 20:1).

Did you know the gospel existed before Jesus? Good news appears in the Old Testament. In the first testament, gospel comes from a messenger who announces peace, salvation, and that the God of Zion rules (Isaiah 52:7). God's good news predates Jesus and prepares for Jesus. A time is coming of peace, good news, salvation, and the rule of God. The gospel announces God's kingdom, the place where God rules and accomplishes his will.

In the second testament or New Testament, "gospel" becomes a familiar word. One of the best descriptions of what gospel means comes in Mark 1:1. The good news is about Jesus Christ. "Jesus" comes from a Hebrew word that means "God saves." "Christ" means king. "Son of God" points to divinity. The good news is *about* Jesus.

Second, the good news is *preached* by Jesus. Jesus proclaims the good news that the time has arrived, the kingdom of God is here, turn your life around, and believe this good news (Mark 1:14–15). The moment all have awaited has arrived. God's kingdom is established now. Once again, the best definition for "gospel" is the good news of what God does that humans cannot do. This good news is about Jesus and also is preached by Jesus as the available rule of God, the kingdom of God.

In Luke 4, Jesus disappears to a deserted place with God. Later, people want him to do "kingly" things. The people always want him to do kingly things—feed, heal, teach, and save them. But Jesus says, "I must proclaim the good news of the kingdom of God; for I was sent for this purpose" (Luke 4:43). How is this "kingdom of God" message good news for us today? The kingdom of God sounds ancient and out of date.

The kingdom of God is the core content of Jesus' preaching. As Jesus walks the earth, he preaches the available rule of God and regularly claims it as his purpose. A few verses earlier, Jesus' first sermon is recorded after his baptism. This is Jesus' first public message after his ministry begins. In Nazareth, he stands to speak in his hometown synagogue. He reads from the prophet Isaiah: "The Spirit of the Lord is upon me, because he has anointed me to bring good news to the poor. He has sent me to proclaim release to the captives . . . and to proclaim the year of the Lord's favor" (Luke 4:18–19; Isa 61:1–2). When he sits to teach, Jesus expresses that this ancient prophecy is fulfilled in this day in their listening. Jesus proclaims himself as the Messiah. They seem to like his message. Then, he opens the door to all humanity—the good news of the kingdom is also for non-Jews. God intends to save the world. Now, they are ready to kill him. What is good news for some is not good news for others. They want to regain exclusive rule. It is not good news to them that God rules for everyone's benefit. However, the kingdom of God is good news for everyone. Good news is for the poor, oppressed outsider. If the gospel is not good news for everyone then it is not good news.

Earlier, Jesus' ministry begins with his baptism and God's confirmation. When John baptizes Jesus, God's spirit comes upon him as a dove and God's voice labels Jesus as "God's son." Immediately after this confirming start to his ministry, Jesus goes into the wilderness. The devil tempts Jesus in the wild. Examined carefully, these temptations from

Satan are not random but threaten Jesus' ministry.[2] They attack the gospel of the kingdom of God (Luke 4:1–13) even though the actions might please the crowds as "kingly." First, the devil encourages Jesus to prove he is king by turning rocks to bread. Kings feed their people. This is an *economic* temptation to be like Moses in the wilderness, bringing people manna bread from heaven. Jesus is tempted to be relevant to immediate needs—feed us what we want and need. Second, the devil offers to give Jesus all the kingdoms of the earth in an instant. Jesus can establish his kingdom through *political* power. This is a temptation to establish the kingdom by power and influence. Satan has armies of people as slaves to his will. The devil easily can provide forces to take and establish political power. The final temptation is to prove kingship by miraculous undeniable *spiritual* means: Jesus, jump from the temple and wow the crowds. Make a religious spectacle that will draw, delight, and amaze people. But Jesus' kingdom is not about relevance, easy power, or religious spectacle. The kingdom of God is established through suffering, sacrifice, and death. Even today, Jesus is considered irrelevant, weak, and uninspiring.

However, the kingdom of God is established by the life of Jesus, the sacrifice of Jesus, and the victory Jesus wins over death. Jesus is our example, our sacrifice, and our salvation. Jesus is the answer to the covenant promise God made to Abraham thousands of years previous. God does not forget his holy covenant sworn to Abraham, calling us to "serve him without fear, in holiness and righteousness before him all our days" (Luke 1:72–75). The covenant is fulfilled in Christ in an amazing good news way but not as anyone expected. Jesus predicted his life was to end in suffering and death. The promise of God is a new covenant in his own blood (Luke 22:20). Who could imagine that death would bring life?

Luke points readers to Jerusalem. This is the city to which Jesus moves with deliberation. Jesus "sets his face toward Jerusalem" (9:51–53; 13:22, 33; 17:11; 18:31; 19:11, 28), because he is determined to go there to die like any good prophet. Jesus' plan is simple: go to Jerusalem and be killed by the world he intends to save. For Jesus, Jerusalem is the city that kills the prophets (Luke 13:33–35). And that is exactly what happens. Jesus is killed by a combination of Jewish authorities, religious figures, and Roman authorities. Everyone abandons Jesus to the cross. This is not good news.

2. Nouwen, In the Name of the Father, 13–70.

Jesus' death in Jerusalem is not the end of the story of God. The story of God is given new life in Jesus' resurrection. This God refuses to let human unfaithfulness, even blatant rejection of God, keep God from showing love. God remains faithful to the promises he gave to Adam in creation, to Abraham with the covenant, and to the world through Jesus Christ. God's story and mission are forever united with the story of humanity. The God who becomes human invites us as human beings to live a divine life that partners with God in this world (2 Peter 1:4).

The mission of God is our mission. Some people may not want another mission in life because we already are full of missions. Plus, God's mission is full of difficult personal sacrifice and humility. God's mission is to get down in the muck of the human pigsty and, as Jesus says, "Seek and save the lost" (Luke 19:10). Christians harvest this verse from the story of a despised tax collector named Zach, who bows to the foreign system to make money. Jesus hangs out with Zach because of this mission of God. The people assume that since Jesus is close to Jerusalem and discussing salvation that the kingdom of God will appear. The kingdom of God does appear, in the human form of Jesus but not as it is expected.

Instead, in Jesus' mission (Luke 24:44–49), the Messiah suffers and dies so that repentance and forgiveness can be proclaimed to all nations. We are witnesses. We have God's spirit. We continue to receive the promises Jesus made to the apostles.

Good news is not religion and not for personal fulfillment. The good news is the dream of another way of life following Jesus. The way of Jesus is the way of death to self in order to find life in the kingdom of God. While Jesus sometimes seems irrelevant, unspectacular, and weak, he shows us how to live with God under the rule of God. God lives among us to connect with us. God rules us to give us life in his kingdom. God sends us on a missionary task to the world.

DAY 2

▷▶ DISCUSS

Small Group Discussion (60 minutes)

This week the reading and small group discussion explore the "incarnation" of Jesus. This small group is an "incarnational" experience of seeing God still at work in human lives. As Jesus lived among us so the Spirit of God continues to live and act among us today. This week open yourself to God's working in every part of your routine.

> **LEADER:** Remember to pray inwardly and silently for group members as they are talking. This will make you more attuned to God's activity in their words.

MOVE 1: SHARING PRAYER CONVERSATION (15 MINUTES)

- For what are you *thankful*?
- How have you *seen God at work*?
- For what are you *sorry*?
- To whom do you *need to show love*?

MOVE 2: LISTENING TO OTHERS' STORIES (30 MINUTES)

- Last week's Echoes activity asked you to observe what people worship or esteem in life. Tell the group something you learned.
- What is the best news you have heard this week?
- Share an experience when you were told surprising information or good news.

> **LEADER:** This practice of "echoing" God's story into people's lives is easier when you pay close attention to and review the *Reading* each week.

MOVE 3: TELLING STORIES (10 MINUTES)

- The Listening Leader articulates connections between the stories told in the session and the story of God from the reading or Scripture.
- For example, use some of the stories shared about good news to connect with how God entering the suffering and sin of this world changes life.

Move 4: Connecting Conversation Prayer (5 minutes)

- This prayer time begins by reciting 1 Kings 8:23 together:

    *O Lord, God of Israel, there is no God like you
    in heaven above or on earth beneath,
    keeping covenant and steadfast love
    for your servants who walk before you with all
    their heart.*

- Leader ends with a prayer that reflects some of the stories and conversations from the group discussion.

> **Leader:**
> Don't forget to practice! Before the group dismisses, describe the Echoes of God activity. Challenge group members to join you in the practice of listening this week.

Days 3—7

▷▷▶ PRACTICE

Echoes of God Activity

This week watch the news or your favorite television show and look for examples of undeserved rescue and how it can change life. Think about a time in your life when you were rescued from disaster or trouble and it was undeserved and unearned.

▷▷▷▶ REFLECT

The Story & My Story

These Scripture readings and questions are for reflection. The first question reflects on the text and the second on "My Story." If you have less time read only the underlined chapter.

Day 3: Luke 1, 2, 3

- What is the social status of the people God uses in this story?
- Who are the "lowly" people in my life?

Week Seven: God Lives Among His People

Day 4: Luke 4–7

- List some characteristics of Jesus' relationship with God.
- What habits or qualities of Jesus' relationship with God could I practice in my relationship with God?

Day 5: Luke 10, 11, 12

- What do Jesus' teachings reveal to me about God's desires?
- What role does (should) prayer play in my life right now?

Day 6: Luke 13, 14, 15, 16

- What do Jesus' parables reveal about God's character?
- Am I concerned about the lost things of God?

Day 7: Luke 22, 23, 24

- How does Jesus' action reveal God's desires?
- How has God's merciful love appeared in my life?

> **REMINDER:** Learning a new skill requires practice. This week's Echoes activity is to listen for people's rescue stories.

8

Week Eight: God Enters Into His People

The story about God entering human history was not merely a onetime event. For an eternal God, the incarnation has eternal significance. As you *Read* and *Discuss*, it should become clear that God's Spirit remains active within people today. Your *Practice* and *Reflection* provide new opportunities to live your life with God in God's story.

DAY 1

▶ READ

The story of Harold Crick in the movie *Stranger than Fiction* is interesting, to say the least. Harold, played by Will Ferrell, discovers that he is the main character in a famous author's next novel. This might be exciting, except Harold discovers the author writes tragedies and always kills the main character in her novels. An English professor, played by Dustin Hoffman, helps Harold locate the author. Harold meets the author, and she is stunned that her fictional character is a real person. She is about to kill him—if she finishes the book. She is overcome that her books may murder people. Harold is overcome that he is about to die.

The English professor reads the novel for Harold. He tells Harold that Harold must die, because the book is a masterpiece. This scene is a metaphor of God and Jesus. Like Jesus, Harold willingly decides to face his death and die to save a boy. The author of the story is shocked that Harold would die willingly. When she wrote the book, it was about a man who died unknowingly. Now he is a man willing to die and "that's the kind of guy we should keep alive." Harold is a Christ-figure in this movie. His willing choice to die saves a little boy from death. The story of

God is hidden in a movie. Jesus willingly chose death in order to rescue humanity from destruction by showing a different way to live.

The problem we face in the story of God today is how to keep Jesus alive. If Jesus shows us what God looks like, then we need to keep Jesus around. The story of God is not something God writes in the sky. God actually enters his story and history. Through Jesus' birth, God dons the starring role. This story is probably not one Hollywood would write for God. God is born an illegitimate child to poor Jews in a barn. His life is virtually unknown except for his brief three-year teaching career. The religious people he should have impressed hate him. Those with political power seem unthreatened by a weak, non-violent, would-be king. God writes himself into history not to reign but to face suffering and death. Jesus' resurrection gives life to God's intentions for creation. Imagine a God who willingly is killed, suffers death, and victoriously defeats sin's power. The only thing sin has going for it is death. We fear death, but God shows that for those who wear the name of Jesus and live the life of Jesus, death is irrelevant!

When God dies—as Jesus—the story reaches its climax and history finds its pivotal point. It is appropriate that years are tracked from this moment in time. Time before Christ is BC, and AD means *ano domini* or in the year of the Lord. The story of God may be pictured from a historical framework. In the first testament, Genesis chapters 1–11 deal with all of humanity. God creates the world. Then, the story focuses on Abraham and his descendants. God uses one man to funnel blessings to the entire world. Jesus, a descendant of Abraham, expands God's blessing to the world. Jesus' ministry focuses on Israel, God's chosen nation, but he often reaches out to non-Jews, Gentiles, half-Jew Samaritans, and anyone who comes his way. According to Luke's gospel, Jesus is pointed straight at Jerusalem, the capital of God's nation where kings reign and God's people worship. Jesus says that Jerusalem kills the prophets sent to it (Luke 13:33). Luke's gospel moves towards Jerusalem. The city is a theological outline that climaxes with the cross and resurrection. The victory of God over sin and death is vital. Luke's sequel book, Acts, moves followers of Jesus from Jerusalem to the world.

Jesus' mission establishes the kingdom of God in his life, suffering, death, and resurrection. Jesus' message preaches the kingdom of God, announcing that God's kingdom has arrived in time and space. In his life, Jesus preaches the good news of the kingdom of God (Luke

4:43) and heals people. Jesus sends his followers on the same mission to proclaim the presence of God's kingdom and to heal (Luke 9:2, 6; 10:9). Jesus moves with deliberation to the cross in Jerusalem, where he dies as the son of God and king of the Jews. After his resurrection, Jesus preaches about the kingdom of God (Acts 1:3). The book of Acts tells the spread of the story. From Jerusalem, the apostles move outward into the entire world. Jesus sends them as witnesses in Jerusalem, Judea, Samaria, and to the ends of the earth (Acts 1:8). This is the pattern for their mission work and the outline of the book. Believers are sent from Jerusalem in the power of the Spirit (1:1—8:3). Jerusalem now becomes the starting line for God's mission to the entire world. Second, the Spirit moves to Judea and Samaria, the immediate countries surrounding Jerusalem. Judea represents pure Jews, and Samaria represents those who compromise the race (8:4—12:25). Finally, the "ends of the earth" refer to the Gentiles, a technical term for anyone not a Jew (Acts 13-28).

There are three stories to engage the Holy Spirit's work from Acts. While often called the "Acts of the Apostles," the apostles are mentioned only thirty times. Actually, only two apostles are discussed in detail: the outspoken fisherman Peter and the adopted apostle Paul. The Holy Spirit is the dominant presence for establishing the church and is mentioned almost seventy times. The "Acts of the Holy Spirit" is a more accurate title.

The first Holy Spirit story is Pentecost (Acts 1-2). Jesus amazes the world by willingly surrendering to arrest, suffering, and death. The disciples are scattered and shocked by this event. Then, three days later Jesus is alive. The resurrected Jesus pops up everywhere in Luke. Acts, the sequel to Luke, begins by telling this ascension story again. Jesus appears over forty days. He orders the apostles to remain in Jerusalem and wait for God to give the Holy Spirit, promising they will be baptized with the Holy Spirit.

The apostles assume the kingdom of God will be established immediately. They are ready to see Israel reestablished as God's nation. Imagine the great reign Jesus would have if he appeared to Pilate or to the Jewish religious authorities. Without question the world would crown him as king. His spectacular appearance would provide irrefutable proof of divinity and kingship. They want to see the kingdom now, but Jesus indicates that desire misses the point. The kingdom of God is not about dates or nations but about the apostles being witnesses. The kingdom of God is something that people enter, live, and share.

The risen *presence* of Jesus tells disciples they will receive the *power* of the Holy Spirit and the result will be their *witnessing* to the world about Jesus (Acts 1:8). Then, Jesus disappears and ascends to his heavenly throne as King of Kings. The apostles stand with mouths gaping at the open sky of his disappearance. Now what? If Jesus wants the kingdom of God to make a difference, then Jesus should stick around. A living, resurrected Jesus is convincing proof that God lives. No one could doubt his kingship. But Jesus leaves. The disciples' first step after seeing Jesus is to wait in prayer. The first step is not establishing a human kingdom in power but watching and praying.

They stay in Jerusalem waiting for a week to ten days. Then, at one gathering, a violent rush of wind fills the room. Fire appears and rests upon each of them. They all breathe in the Holy Spirit and begin to speak in foreign languages. At Pentecost, Jews gather in Jerusalem to celebrate the Feast of Weeks and remember the giving of the Torah to Moses on Sinai. Pentecost means "fifty," and it is the fiftieth day after Passover. Jews are each able to hear in their home language. On this Pentecost, something momentous occurs. A long, long time ago at the tower of Babel, all languages were confused and the world was separated. On this Pentecost, the languages unite, and people hear the same message. The apostle Peter addresses an awed crowd about their experience. Peter reads from the Prophet Joel 2:28–32 (see also Acts 2:17–21), where God promised to pour out the Spirit of God upon all flesh, sons and daughters, young and old, female slaves and male slaves. This Pentecost moment is a profound beginning to God's presence among his people. God first lives among us as Jesus, but now God lives inside us.

Nationality makes no difference for inclusion in God's nation. Neither does gender nor social standing matter. The Holy Spirit is not restricted to Jesus. The Spirit present at Jesus' baptism is now present in our lives. The Holy Spirit is a gift. This must have astounded Jews who thought God was interested only in them. Now, God lives in anyone who seeks first his kingdom and accepts his kingship. Or, as Joel and Peter say, "Everyone who calls upon the name of the Lord will be saved" (Joel 2:32; Acts 2:21).

Now that Jesus arrives in the story of God, all the promises made to Abraham are complete. The one remaining promise is to bless all nations through Abraham. Abraham's descendant Jesus is a son of David, pronounced the king of the Jews. After Jesus' ascension, the Holy Spirit of God completes the promise of God's abiding presence. In addition to Joel, the prophet Ezekiel foretold this time when God would put his spirit in us and give life (Ezekiel 37:13–14). The Spirit is God's presence in life. God is available to us. There is neither a priest between you and God nor a temple wall. No nationality, social status, nor gender separates humans from God. God is available.

The second important story in the Acts of the Holy Spirit comes in chapter 10 with the gift of the Spirit to Cornelius and his family. Cornelius is an Italian man who serves as a Roman centurion. He is a Gentile, not part of the nation of Israel, yet Cornelius worships Yahweh. He is devout, prays Jewish prayers, and gives to the needy. Cornelius and his household are known as "God-fearers," or Yahweh worshipers.

One afternoon at 3 p.m., Cornelius dreams that a messenger walks into his house and calls, "Cornelius." He is terrified. The messenger tells him to send for Peter, who is staying with a Gentile named Simon the Tanner. Jews are not supposed to stay with Gentiles, and they certainly do not live with Gentiles who tan animal skins, making them ritually unclean. Cornelius sends one of his devout, God-fearing soldiers along with two slaves thirty miles to Joppa.

The next day, Peter is praying while waiting for lunch. He falls asleep and dreams about food lowered from heaven on a picnic sheet. Peter is hungry and may have smelled the aroma of food in the Gentile neighborhood. However, the sheet is filled with food he has never eaten because of God's commands. These exotic dishes are foods banned from Jewish menus. This picnic is offered by a voice, "Eat up, Peter." Being a good clean Jew, Peter refuses the offer. However, the voice says, "What God calls clean, you must not call profane." Three times Peter is invited to eat. Then, the Spirit tells Peter to get up and meet three Gentile men at the door. Peter goes with the men to see Cornelius.

By the time Peter arrives at Cornelius' home a large gathering of family has assembled. Peter and Cornelius exchange dreams and are stunned that God brings them together. Peter begins to preach that God treats every nationality with equity. God wants all people to follow him. Peter shares how Jesus was anointed by God with his Holy Spirit and appeared to witness and share the message of Jesus as good news for all people (Acts 10:34–48). He conveys how Jesus showed the power of God and preached the peace of God. Although Jesus was killed by humanity, says Peter, God raised him to life. Peter explains how he and other apostles and disciples have had the special privilege of being witnesses to Jesus.

The Holy Spirit falls upon everyone listening. The Holy Spirit *is not restricted to Jews*. The Holy Spirit infuses Gentiles that are not yet circumcised or even baptized as Christians. It is astounding when God works outside the expected order. Some believe there is one specific order or pattern for salvation: belief, repentance, baptism, and the Holy Spirit gift. These circumcised Jewish followers of Jesus are dumbfounded that the Spirit comes to non-Jews. Probably, there is discussion about whether the Gentiles need to be circumcised as full-fledged Jews before becoming Christians, but this is irrelevant since they already have the Spirit. The Holy Spirit is a gift for all people. Enemy outsiders are no longer outsiders. They are insiders.

The final Holy Spirit story comes from the last section of Acts, where the gospel is sent to the ends of the earth (chapters 13–28). Paul and Barnabas face Judeans who demand Gentiles be circumcised before becoming Christians (Acts 15:1). Paul and Barnabas have a blowout argument with them. It is so controversial that they agree to go to Jerusalem and talk it over with the council. The Jerusalem council is a group of founding apostles and elders in the church, who make decisions. While Paul and Barnabas are welcomed, the Pharisee Christians demand that all Gentiles be circumcised.

Peter identifies himself as a missionary to the Gentiles. He explains how God gave his Spirit to Gentiles, making absolutely no distinction between Gentiles and Jews (Acts 15:6–11). What the early church witnesses is no small thing. The Jews believe pagan Gentiles lack the necessary moral and religious background and fear that Gentile entry into the church might be detrimental. However, Peter, Paul, and others testify that the Gentiles do not need circumcision as an outward sign of faith. These Gentiles fear God, give alms, pray, and show God's presence in their lives. Peter preaches that God's plan from the beginning is for the world. He quotes the prophet Amos, saying God plans to rebuild the temple for the Jews and for "all the nations called by my name" (Amos 9:11–12; Acts 15:17). The kingdom of God is open to all people.

The Holy Spirit will not be restricted to external ritual. The Jerusalem council determines the physical act of circumcision is no longer a requirement for Gentile believers. Instead, Gentiles show the presence of God's Spirit by eliminating idolatrous practices like meat sacrificed to idols and pagan sexual activity. God's covenant mark of circumcision is set aside in order to show God's astounding grace. Circumcision no longer marks a boundary; the Holy Spirit is boundary marker enough.

Salvation comes through the grace of God to all. Even Jews cannot keep the law perfectly (Acts 15:10–11). God's grace has been lifted over religious ritual. The Holy Spirit is a gift given to all people who seek God. Today, we often esteem religious practice more than people, yet all people receive the same grace of God.

The book of Acts ends with Paul preaching in Rome about "the good news of the kingdom of God" and Jesus Christ (Acts 28:23–24, 31). God's message is given by Jesus in Jerusalem and now through the apostles to the ends of the earth. Jesus leaves earth to enable others as witnesses. Jesus' mission of spreading the message of the kingdom is kept alive through our spirit-filled living. God does not write this story detached from reality like the author in *Stranger than Fiction*. Jesus is alive in the hearts and lives of disciples dedicated to the kingdom of God. God's Spirit and God's story live on in us.

The story of God becomes our story, because Jesus turns God's story into a human story. The movement of the Spirit shows this throughout the Bible. The Holy Spirit is present in creation (Genesis 1:1) and breathes life into Adam. At Jesus' baptism, the Holy Spirit descends on Jesus and God identifies Jesus as God's son. At Pentecost, the Spirit descends upon the followers of Jesus. The arrival of the Holy Spirit unites the human and divine stories. Jesus remains at work in this world through the Holy Spirit of God alive in us. The Holy Spirit enables people to testify that God reigns and his kingdom has come. The Holy Spirit comes upon men and women, employees and bosses, Jews and non-Jews. God's kingdom is one of equality in Christ (Galatians 3:28). The Spirit works through our actions of living the fruit of the Spirit (Galatians 5:22–23). The Spirit uses our words to witness that the kingdom of God has arrived for the salvation of all people (Romans 3:22-23).

The Holy Spirit is not restricted to Jesus or Jews or the super-religious but is God's gift to all people. In 2 Corinthians 3:18, Paul writes how all of us may see "the glory of the Lord as though reflected in a mirror, [as we] are being transformed into the same image from one degree of glory to another; for this comes from the Lord, the Spirit." The Holy Spirit transforms us into the image of Christ one degree at a time. The Holy Spirit is a gift given to all people who seek God without ritual burdens.

Our stories are connected as human beings and also as children of God. Jesus remains alive today through Holy Spirit believers who live as God's children. We no longer live separate lives but live connected together by God's own Spirit. This knowledge of God's kingdom and mission requires us to enter the world and connect with God's children who do not yet know the grand story of God's love for all people.

Day 2

▷▶ DISCUSS

Small Group Discussion (60 minutes)

Move 1: Sharing Prayer Conversation (15 minutes)

- For what are you *thankful*?
- How have you *seen God at work*?
- For what are you *sorry*?
- To whom do you *need to show love*?

> **Leader:**
> Remember to pray inwardly and silently for group members as they are talking. This will make you more attuned to God's activity in their words.

Move 2: Listening to Others' Stories (30 minutes)

- Invite people to share their "Echoes of God" experiences about an undeserved rescue from last week.
- Tell a story of how being in an uncomfortable or new place (group or country) impacted you.
- Describe the settings (and people) where you go to feel most at home (peaceful, comfortable).

Move 3: Telling Stories (10 minutes)

- The Listening Leader articulates connections between the stories told in the session and the story of God from the reading or Scripture.
- For example, a leader might take the group's stories about a soul feeding event or their experience of God in an uncomfortable

place and compare or contrast it with Paul and Peter's surprising experiences of God.

Move 4: *Connecting Conversation Prayer* (5 minutes)

- This prayer time begins by reciting 1 Kings 8:23 together:

  O Lord, God of Israel, there is no God like you
  in heaven above or on earth beneath,
  keeping covenant and steadfast love
  for your servants who walk before you with all
  their heart.

- Leader ends with a prayer that reflects some of the stories and conversations from the group discussion.

> **Leader:**
> Before the group dismisses, choose the best one of the two Echoes of God activities for your group. Encourage the group to practice listening this week.

Days 3—7

▷▷▶ PRACTICE

Echoes of God Activity

Activity 1: Go to a public place you normally do not go. The place needs to be somewhere a bit uncomfortable for you, where the majority of the people are of a different social class from you (i.e. upper, lower, or middle class). Spend 30-60 minutes watching and praying for all the people you see. Prepare for God to surprise you.

or

Activity 2: Follow Activity 1 (above) but make conversation with people. Focus your conversation on them and their interests. Avoid talking about yourself. Instead, listen to their stories.

Week Eight: God Enters Into His People 77

▷▷▷▶ REFLECT

The Story & My Story

These Scripture readings and questions are for reflection. Question one reflects on the text and the second on "My Story." If you have less time read only the underlined chapter.

Day 3: Acts 1, 2, 3

- What things surprise you about the early church?
- What part of the early church do you desire to recapture?

Day 4: Acts 4–6

- In what ways does God's Spirit rule the life of Peter and John?
- How does God reign over my life?

Day 5: Acts 7–8

- What is powerful about Stephen's sermon?
- How would I relate the story of God's salvation to a friend (story, song, movie, experience)?

> **Reminder:**
> The Echoes activity asks you to spend an hour in a place you do not normally go to pray, observe, and possibly interact with people. Add this as an event in your calendar.

Day 6: Acts 9, 10–12

- What does God's action toward non-Jews teach me about my actions toward non-Christians?
- How have you seen God work in a non-believer's life?

Day 7: Acts 13–15

- To whom does God give gifts?
- Who are the "outsiders" or outcasts in my life?

9

Week Nine: God Preaches the Gospel to Everyone

This week the story of God takes a biographical look at the Jewish leader Saul who became an apostle of Jesus. This *Reading* about Saul gives an unorthodox look at his life and writings. The group *Discussion*, *Reflection*, and *Practice* invite participants to see their lives like Paul's life—part of God's ongoing story.

DAY 1

▶ READ

The story of the world today is war. We battle in religion, politics, and economics. Terrorism attacks Western power, religion, and wealth. The people of the world dislike the worldwide power, wealth, and influence of America.

Once there was a religious radical willing to kill for his belief in God. His guerrilla tactics threatened murder or imprisonment to any who claimed Jesus as Lord (Acts 9:1-2). While not a suicide bomber, this terrorist observed the execution of Christians. He planned attacks on them. His intention was the complete destruction of Christianity by imprisoning and executing followers of Jesus one by one (Galatians 1:13, 23). Amazingly, this highly educated terrorist lived this way to honor God and preserve the purity of his religion. His terrorist leanings were backed by strong religious fervor and doctrine.

Imagine inviting him to speak in America. It is difficult to imagine being in the same room with someone who executes Christians and intends to exterminate all Christians in a Christian holocaust. No one would sit beside him. However, this terrorist has a conversion experience like Osama Bin Laden becoming Billy Graham. Osama, who rejoices in

American deaths, converts to Christianity, and becomes a more influential evangelist than Billy Graham. While hard to imagine, the terrorist described has this type of extreme transformation. One day he is chasing Christians to Damascus to extradite them to Jerusalem for trial. Then, a penetrating light drives him to the ground. A booming voice confronts him, "Saul, Saul why are you persecuting me?" This Jew named Saul fearfully replies, "Who are you Lord?" The voice's response alters the course of Saul's life, saying, "I am Jesus whom you are persecuting." This story of Saul's transformation is told three separate times in Acts (9:3–8; 22:6–11; 26:12–19). Saul mentions his radical transformation twice in his letters (Galatians 1:12–24; 1 Cor 15:8).

Saul (or Paul) is a devoted, religious radical Jew, who loves God passionately. Paul has a unique nationality. Paul is from Tarsus on the southeastern coast of Turkey. His parents are Diaspora Jews, dispersed outside their Palestinian homeland due to the multiple captivities of God's people to foreign power. However, they remain practicing Jews. Their son has two names, one Greek (Paul) and one Hebrew (Saul) that reveal his unique experience. Alexander the Great brought Greek culture to the world, stripping countries of their original cultures. However, some Jews hung on to faith and tradition.

Paul's family traces their Jewish ancestry to the tribe of Benjamin. Paul is raised a good Jewish boy. He is tattooed with God's covenant to Abraham by being circumcised on the eighth day (Philippians 3:3–6). He attends Jewish synagogue in Tarsus. This talented young man is taken to Jerusalem, the pinnacle of Jewish faith and education, to be a disciple of Rabbi Gamaliel (Acts 22:3; 5:34). Gamaliel is the grandson of the famous rabbi Hillel, a founder of the Pharisee sect. Paul is impressive. His knowledge and practice of the Law of Moses is above question. He joins the strictest Jewish sect, known as the Pharisees, "the set apart" or super-duper holy ones. It is also likely that Paul sits on the Sanhedrin, the Jewish Ruling council. His religious and political zeal make him willing to persecute and kill Christians in the name of God. Paul is a Jew who is going places. He is on the "God track," until God shows up and turns Paul's clarity, order, and esteem upside down. Jesus was not a fake Messiah. Jesus was not simply an uneducated, Nazarene carpenter. Jesus was God's son, the Jewish Messiah, and the King of all Kings. God decides it is time Paul recognize Jesus.

From this moment, Paul is transformed from a persecuting opponent to an advocating disciple of Jesus. The lightening-flash conversation with Jesus leaves Paul blind for three days. He waits in Damascus. Paul cannot read the Law of Moses, which does not matter because he has it memorized. Instead, Paul probably reflects upon the law in his heart and tries to make sense of all that has happened. Ananias, a disciple in Damascus, has the misfortune of a vision from God that sends him to Paul, the number one enemy of Jesus. God restores Paul's sight through Ananias. Paul is filled with the Holy Spirit. Then, Paul is baptized. Paul meets with other disciples in Damascus. Immediately, he begins proclaiming that Jesus is the son of God in the Jewish synagogues. Paul spends three years in Arabia, hidden from Jews who now want to kill him and from Christians, uncertain about his supposed "transformation." Paul spends decades as an adopted apostle of Jesus to the Gentiles (Galatians 1:15–16, 2:7–8), traveling the well-paved Roman roads to the key cities of Greece and Asia Minor. Paul goes to large population centers and speaks in synagogues or anywhere the crowds gather.

Paul's experience with Jesus significantly impacts all of Christianity and Judaism. Paul becomes an apostle of Jesus. The adopted apostle label comes from Paul's statement in 1 Corinthians 15:8–9 about being the "unnaturally born apostle." In the introduction of almost every letter, Paul goes by the title "apostle." Clearly, Paul is the fourteenth apostle. His significant influence can be read in his thirteen letters to churches, which form half the New Testament. His message is the same as the other apostles. He preaches the gospel of God about Jesus the King, who is full of the spirit and holiness. In Romans 1:1–7, Paul describes the gospel of God by connecting the Old Testament promises of God with the contemporary life of Jesus Christ. For Paul, faith in Jesus Christ shows God's righteousness. Martin Luther, the Christian Reformer, was drawn to these words:

> For I am not ashamed of the gospel; it is the power of God for the salvation to everyone who has faith, to the Jew first and also to the Greek. For in it the righteousness of God is revealed through faith for faith; as it is written, "The one who is righteous will live by faith." (Romans 1:16–17)

Paul summarizes the story of God as good news for everyone with faith, both Jews and non-Jews. This message is for all people and not just a select group. God's righteousness comes to live in those with faith in

Jesus. The good news message of God's grace appears in 1 Corinthians 15. The gospel message Paul receives and passes on is that the Messiah died for our sins, was buried, raised, and appeared to many. God's grace leads to proclaiming that message and inspiring belief (1 Corinthians 15:10–11).

Paul writes no first-century book or autobiography but only letters to churches. One such letter is the story of Romans about "who is saved," and another is the story of Ephesians about "the mystery." The story of Romans is Paul's longest and possibly greatest letter. Unlike his other letters, Paul writes to a church not yet visited. He longs to help this church with Jews and Gentiles at the ends of the earth. Paul writes to introduce himself and to address the hostility between Jew and Gentile Christians.

God places the uniquely talented Paul at a specific point in God's story. Paul's Jewish pedigree is outstanding. Paul also has a strong Greek pedigree. He is a natural-born Roman citizen, considered the best citizenship in the world. There are times Paul withholds mention of his citizenship to escape special treatment. Other times he mentions his citizenship to further the cause of Jesus. Paul speaks to Jews and Gentiles with authority. The greeting he uses in every letter is this: "Grace and Peace." "Grace" means "gift" and sounds like the Greek word for "greeting." "Peace" is the Greek word used for the Jewish greeting "Shalom," a theological concept for the peace God establishes. Even in a greeting, Paul reaches to both cultures.

Imagine an early house church gathering. The large living room is split into the Northside Jewish Church and the Southside Gentile church. Paul's letter is read aloud as a sermon. After Paul introduces himself and the gospel (Romans 1:1–17), he immediately addresses the issue. The Gentiles are the problem. They do not recognize God. So, God allows their corrupted minds to destroy them as a consequence of their actions (Romans 1:28, 20–21). Paul strongly critiques the average pagan Gentile living in wickedness, idol worship, and sexual freedom. As we look around that living room, the Northside Jewish Christians are nodding and smirking, "It is about time that someone brought morals to these pagans." The Gentile Christians frown and squirm in their seats.

Then, as chapter 2 is read the mood reverses. Like separate thermostat controls in a car, one side feels the heat; now the other side feels it, too. Paul's imaginary finger now points at the Jews. You have no excuse when you judge others, because you condemn yourselves (Romans 2:1). God's righteousness does not come to people who *hear* the law or *know* the law, but God's righteousness justifies those who *do* the law (Romans 2:13). Paul scolds Jews who preach and teach and know the law but break it. He takes circumcision, the physical sign of God's covenant promise to Abraham, and redefines it spiritually. Circumcision is a matter of the heart, and a Jew is a Jew first from the heart (Romans 2:29). The room temperature equalizes. Now both are steamed.

The problem is with Jews and Gentiles, because both are under the power of sin. "There is no one righteous not even one" (Romans 3:9–10). God shows no favoritism or elitism. Humans are all the same. No one is in a position to claim righteousness because all have sinned (Romans 3:21–23).

Two concepts are important: the righteousness of God and the Law of Moses. First, the righteousness of God is unveiled for all to see and for everyone to enjoy. God's righteousness is given through faith in Christ Jesus. God is righteous. We believe God. Second, the law is a hot topic for Paul. But what does he mean by law? The *Torah* is the Mosaic Law given at Sinai. Torah refers to the first five books of Hebrew Scripture sometimes called by the Greek title *Pentateuch*, meaning five containers. The law might refer to the *Tanak* or the entire Hebrew Scriptures comprising the Torah, Prophets, and Writings. Paul may mean the *Mishnah*, the oral commentary on the law, which was later written down and called the *Talmud*. The law at times means each of these. The law had become a *prescriptive* means "to get right with God" instead of *descriptive* of how "God's people live right." People assume the law is righteousness. In other words, somehow law becomes the means by which one become righteous before God.

Paul changes how the law is understood because of Jesus. The "righteousness of God" is not measured by what one does or does not do but by faith in God's righteousness. The purpose of the law is to reflect our failures and give us knowledge of our sin (Romans 3:20; 7:7). The law does not save us. God saves us. The law shows us our sinfulness. The law does not reveal our righteousness but reveals our unrighteousness. To summarize Romans: all humans live in the same story of sin. No matter how good or evil, we are sinners. The law reflects the depths of our sinfulness and our powerlessness to save ourselves. Jesus is the universal savior of all people. We receive the righteousness of God by faith in God's righteousness. Our faith is expressed in a baptismal death in water. We are raised with Christ who gives us new life that shares in God's righteousness. Sin no longer has power over us, because we are under God's grace and not under the law (Romans 6:14). We live righteous. We are living sacrifices. We live in a new story.

The story of Ephesians releases the hidden secret of life. This world is a wrestling match between good and evil. Life is a struggle between life and death. The human body uniquely weaves the physical and spiritual. Through Ephesians we discover that the mystery holding all of life together is Jesus Christ. God's plan was founded before the world began: to gather up all things spiritual and physical, heavenly and earthly in Jesus (Ephesians 1:4, 9–10). Jesus is our destiny (v. 11). Every human—regardless of nationality, gender, race, or religion—finds his or her completion in Jesus.

This little letter of mysteries combines what we *believe* (chapters 1–3) with how we *live* (chapters 4–6) in Jesus Christ. Belief in Jesus may not be separated from behaving like Jesus. The letter's first three chapters describe our selection as children of Jesus Christ. Humans are chosen before the world's creation to be children of God (1:11–14). But few people believe that God has all humans in mind. Paul's experience exemplifies how we must learn that God's promises include every human being. Paul grows up as a "chosen" insider of God. Paul believes his view of God is the exclusively correct view. However, he and fellow Jews miss the point: being insider to God's promises means blessing other nations rather than privilege over others. The prophet Isaiah explained that Israel was light to the nations (or Gentiles), so God's salvation could reach the whole earth (Isa 49:6). God's promise has everyone in view. Being an insider does not mean knowing the law, practicing ritual, or doing the right things. Ephesians chapters 1–3 tell the story of belief in the mystery of Christ as good news for everyone.

The second half of the Ephesians story is about living (chapters 4–6). Belief in Jesus enables the behavior of Jesus. Humans now are free to live in humility, gentleness, patience, love (4:1–5), and not mere ritual. Our belief that Jesus is king and Lord and savior allows us to behave morally, but behavior does not save us. Neither does belief save us. God saves us through the life and salvation of Jesus.

Ephesians relates the human story simply. We think we are alive. We go where we wish, buy what we want, watch what we want, and inject what we want. But we are dead, spiritually dead by sin (2:1–3). We are corpses, stumbling through a lifeless existence.

But, God makes us alive (2:4–6). From the very beginning of time and creation God is about life. He creates you. God knew you before you took shape in the womb. God gives life. We create death by avoiding God. We dig our own grave of sin and lay down in it. However, God digs us up and gives us life.

We are God's masterpiece (2:7–10). God saves us by grace (v. 8). No matter what we have done and in spite of what we have not done, God thinks of us as his masterpieces. He gives us grace, mercy, and love. We still may choose death. God wants us to choose life. His eternal life is a gift by grace through faith.

We can learn a lot from a Palestinian terrorist named Paul (or Saul). First, God can change and transform anyone, turning terrorists into evangelists of his good news message for all people. Second, the story of the Roman letter is that God saves all people through faith in Jesus Christ. The gospel shows God's righteousness for everyone. Finally, the Ephesian letter teaches how God reveals the secret life in Jesus. Though dead spiritually, God makes us alive as masterpiece witnesses to the world. We are enabled to truly live.

Day 2

▷▶ DISCUSS

Small Group Discussion (60 minutes)

Move 1: *Sharing* Prayer Conversation (15 minutes)

- For what are you *thankful*?
- How have you *seen God at work*?
- For what are you *sorry*?
- To whom do you *need to show love*?

Move 2: *Listening to Others' Stories* (30 minutes)

- Ask group members to relate experiences with the Echoes experiment of watching and praying for people.

- When you were growing up did you see your family as a gift or a burden? How has your childhood made you the person you are today?

- Do the optional exercise in the *Practice* section of this chapter.

> **Leader:**
> Notice the optional exercise below in the Practice section. The exercise may be used as preparation for this week's Echoes of God activity.

Move 3: *Telling* Stories (10 minutes)

- The Listening Leader articulates connections between the stories shared in the session and the story of God from the reading or Scripture.

- The leader may make use of the story of adopted apostle Paul and his experience of Jesus as a connection to the stories people share in this group.

Move 4: *Connecting* Conversation Prayer (5 minutes)

- This prayer time begins by reciting 1 Kings 8:23 together:

  O Lord, God of Israel, there is no God like you
  in heaven above or on earth beneath,
  keeping covenant and steadfast love
  for your servants who walk before you with all their heart.

- Leader ends with a prayer that reflects some of the stories and conversations from the group discussion.

Days 3—7

▷▷▶ PRACTICE

Echoes of God Activity

Activity 1: Notice which people irritate you, anger you, disgust you, or frustrate you. Become aware of people who turn you off. As you realize your resistance to these people, pray for them in the silence of your heart. Pray something like, "God, thank you for this person whom you created in love as a masterpiece for good works" (Ephesians 2:10).

Or if there is time use this group exercise as preparation for the activity.

Group Exercise: Hand out slips of paper and ask people to write down their greatest weakness. This will not be shared with anyone. Read Romans 3:21–24 and Philippians 3:7–11. Then, write a personal strength. Remark that we are not saved because of our strengths nor condemned by our weaknesses. We are saved by the righteousness of God. We live by the righteousness of God. Pass the paper to the person on your left. Everyone shreds the paper and tosses it in the trash and says together, "Saved by God's righteousness."

▷▷▷▶ REFLECT

The Story & My Story

These Scripture readings and questions are for daily reflection. The first question reflects on the text and the second on "My Story." If you have less time read only the underlined chapter.

Day 3: Romans 1–4

- How has God revealed his righteousness to humanity?
- In what ways do I act as if I "have it all together?"

> **REMINDER:**
>
> In this week's Echoes of God activity monitor your anger and irritation. Who irritates you?

Day 4: Romans 9, 10, 11, 12

- What is God's desire or plan for Israel?
- How should I treat Jews (or Gentiles) in my life?

Day 5: 1 Corinthians 9–13

- What is the importance of spiritual discipline?
- How do I spend time "training" for spiritual discipline?

Day 6: 2 Corinthians 2, 3–6

- From where does competence come?
- When do I long for others to notice my strengths and not my weaknesses?

Day 7: Ephesians 1–3

- List the actions that God accomplishes in this text.
- Is it difficult or easy for me to believe that I am "chosen" by God? Why?

10

Week Ten: God's Covenant is Life in Christ

The story of God extends the life of Jesus through the lives of Jesus' disciples and the writings of the apostles. While Christianity gained structure as it spread, the Scriptures reveal disciples committed to living the life of Christ. *Read* the chapter, *Discuss* life with your group, *Practice* listening for God in his people today, and *Reflect* on where God is challenging you to go in discipleship to Jesus.

Day 1

▶ READ

The story of God is written every day. With each new baby conceived, the plot continues. God's work expressed as human life is conceived, comes into being through birth, grows, lives, and dies. Babies receive life as a gift, not by choice. They are born into a story already being narrated.

God is creator of Adam and Eve. God is covenant maker with Abraham for the blessing of the world. The unfortunate human response to the genius of God's drama is the rejection, displacement, and denial of God. Mostly humans ignore God. Little do *we* know, God continues writing us into his love story. The pinnacle moment, of course, is when God writes himself into our story. The moment of Jesus' birth, life, death, and resurrection is paramount in embracing our stories in God.

The New Testament portion of the story narrates the life of Jesus, the Holy Spirit's indwelling activity, the spirit-led work of Paul, and how God's Spirit remains at work in disciples. However, life after Jesus initiates a big change for early disciples. Today many churches and Christians obsess with the finer points of *becoming* a Christian. Few give serious focus to *living* a disciple's life. The apostles show how to live as disciples of Jesus without Jesus being visibly present.

Following Jesus leads disciples through a few phases. At first, a disciple's life is directed by the movement of the Spirit. Everything is new. Churches form. New concepts emerge. Disciples are now making disciples. Second, the disciples continue the rapid expansion of discipleship to the world of Gentiles. There are challenges in gathering all people under the Lordship of Jesus. Third, the church, Christianity, and discipleship to Jesus show a more established life in the Spirit. Jesus' return does not come as quickly as Paul or the apostles hope. Life post-Jesus lasts longer than anyone anticipates. These phases of development after Jesus are recorded in the documents of the New Testament. The oldest documents are Paul's letters. Next oldest are the gospels and more recent are the General or Catholic Epistles (the New Testament letters not written by Paul from Philemon through Jude).

The General Epistles reveal a more structured church. They show how communities of Christians ordered their lives around the new life found in Jesus. Rather than being specific letters to address the unique needs of a church, the general epistles more broadly focus on the universal needs of the growing movement. These letters seem to concentrate on church order. High emphasis is placed upon morality and living as a follower of Jesus. Often they are dated later in the first-century, when Christianity becomes more settled. The story of God continues through the growth of Christianity.

A number of historical events provide the background story for the development of Christianity after Jesus' ascension and through the first-century. The Jewish temple in Jerusalem is destroyed in 70 AD by Titus. Forty years earlier, Jesus predicted the temple's destruction. During the Jew's Great Revolt, the temple becomes a fortress hideout. The Jews are convinced God will save them. Titus tries but fails to get the Jews out of the temple without destroying the temple. The temple is pulled to the ground and burned by Titus and the Tenth Legion during the Great Revolt. This temple's smoldering ruins means the end of temple sacrifices. The temple's Western Wall remains a place of prayer today. The location of worship is altered forever, as Jesus predicts. From this time on Jesus is the one sacrifice for all.

For Jews, the story of God again seems destroyed. The crisis of the temple's destruction leads to the council at Jamnia in 90 AD. This Jewish council is composed of Pharisees, the only remaining Jewish sect. The council sets the canon or list of the Hebrew Scriptures. "Canon" means rule or measuring stick and indicates the books measured as authoritative Scripture. The canon is established using two principles: the prophetic era ended with Ezra and Nehemiah, and only books originally composed in Hebrew are accepted. The council also begins prayer practices to replace sacrifices. Three times each day Jews pray. They face Jerusalem to speak the 18 Benedictions or *Amidah*, meaning "standing prayer," in lieu of temple sacrifices. These enhancements or adjustments to Jewish faith are response to Christianity. Until this time Christianity is considered another sect of Judaism. Christians viewed themselves as Jews. However, Jews see vast differences that call for distinction. From this point, Christianity and Judaism become separate faiths with shared resources. The resources of God's covenant expand to include new documents.

Christians recognize the Hebrew Scriptures as their Scripture. The New Testament is not assembled officially until the fourth-century. Up to this point, the Old Testament functions as Scripture. However, the letters and books of the New Testament are used to help communities of Christians embody the gospel of Jesus Christ in new ways. After Jesus' ascension, and as time passes, the church becomes more organized. This church order is reflected in the eight General Epistles. This chapter explores how the story of God continues through people associated with Jesus: his apostles John and Peter, Jesus' brothers James and Jude, and an anonymous person who preaches the sermon called Hebrews.

Often called the beloved apostle, John was one of Jesus' three closest apostles. John writes a gospel, the intimidating Revelation (inspected next week), and three little love letters. John encourages Christian readers to live in love. Love is the virtue that is supposed to be the identifying trait of Christians. As we live the life of Christ within this longstanding covenant of God, we mirror the love of God (1 John 4:7–10). Love is the last name of Christians. Love is our birthmark. To the degree we show love to one another and to the world is the degree that people see God within us (John 13:35). The story of God is a story of God's persistent love. To live in God's story is to practice love's way by how we order churches, run businesses, and treat fellow moms in PTA.

The apostle Peter was also one of Jesus' prayer partners. He is an outspoken "rock" of a man. Late in his life, Peter's two epistles reveal seasoned wisdom about what life with Jesus looks like. Christians are to be holy. Like God is holy and as Jesus lived in holiness, we are set apart by our conduct of life. Decisions and actions reveal a deeper holiness.

Simply put, Peter says we should be holy (1 Peter 1:13–16). Preparation and discipline get our minds ready for action. It is easy to take instruction from this world, but Peter commands separation from the world's way of thinking and acting. Holiness begins in the heart and is displayed in action. Few people value holiness. Even Christians do not wish to appear "holier than thou," yet living in Christ sets disciples apart from undisciplined living.

Jesus had younger brothers and sisters (Mark 3:32). His brothers were not believers and actually made fun of Jesus for claiming to be the Messiah (John 7:3–4). Who would believe it if their brother claimed to be God in the flesh? That would call for dog-piling, giving a head burn to, or ostracizing this brother. It is not until after Jesus' death and resurrection that Jesus' brothers become believers. Specifically, it takes Jesus appearing to his brother James (1 Corinthians 15:7) for him to believe but believe he does. James becomes a pillar in the church. Surprisingly, James, and not Peter, is the paramount decision maker of the Jerusalem council of apostles (Acts 15:13, 19). James writes an epistle and does not even identify himself as Jesus' brother but as the servant of the Lord Jesus Christ. In this way, James shows he is a true disciple.

James writes about the suffering that will come to believers in Jesus. He writes in a style similar to the "Sermon on the Mount." Among many things, James calls Christians to be single-minded in their endurance and faithfulness (James 1:1–4). James teaches endurance of suffering with joy and faithfulness. Suffering and persecution come to James. He becomes a Christian martyr in 61 AD because of his leadership. James' leadership is actually "follower-ship." James follows Jesus as his Lord.

Jesus' other brother was named Jude. His short, twenty-five-verse letter has the distinction of being the last letter before the more famous Revelation of John. Jude, like his brother James, does not scream, "Hey, I am a brother of Jesus!" Jude identifies himself as a "slave" of Jesus Christ and a brother of James. These two brothers know Jesus is much more than a brother. Although an illegitimate son of Joseph, Jesus is the son of God. By the late first-century, Jesus had become a doctrine to dismiss rather than Lord to follow (Jude 3–4). The faith for which Christians contend against all odds is the grace of God expressed in Jesus as the only Master, Lord, and King. Jude says to live in grace. Contending for the faith does not mean protecting various traditions or rituals. Contending for faith is not about following the law but about the protection of the grace presented in the person of Jesus as Lord.

The story of one final letter is a long anonymous sermon in elaborate Greek, quoting from all over the Hebrew Scriptures. Hebrews is preached to encourage struggling second-generation Christians (Hebrews 2:1-3) who are discouraged (Hebrews 12:1-2, 12-13). The longer people wait for Jesus' return and the longer life's difficulties overwhelm them, it becomes difficult to continue in faith. People doubt that Jesus was the one king and believe he may not return.

God is the hero in Hebrews. This sermon focuses on God's covenant promises and how they are fulfilled in Jesus Christ. The Bible is a storybook of God's promises. In fact, the whole Bible story can be told through God's covenant promises. God creates the world. He gives humans the obligation to work the soil and the freedom to eat the fruit of any tree except the tree of "knowledge of good and evil," which leads to death (Genesis 2:15-17; 3:1-7). Humans break this covenant. After the flood, God promises Noah never to destroy the earth with water, signing this covenant with a rainbow. He obligates humans not to murder or eat blood (Genesis 8:20—9:17). Humans break covenant. Next, God promises to bless Abraham by making his offspring into a huge nation, granting them land, being their God, and blessing all people and nations through Abraham's nation (Genesis 12). The circumcision of males is a sign of the covenant. Based upon his deliverance of Israel from Egypt, God promises to bless Israel as his treasured nation through the Law of Moses and Ten Commandments (Exodus 19:4-6). In return, Israel lives obedient as God's royal nation. Next, God promises to establish King David's throne forever and that God's steadfast love will remain with David forever (2 Samuel 7:12-16; 1 Samuel 8:5-8). After the many failings of the people to keep covenant, God promises through the prophets a new covenant that is written upon the human heart (Jeremiah 31:31-34). Unlike earlier covenants that people break, God forgives and forgets all sin, writing this covenant upon the heart. Finally, through Jesus, God announces a covenant in his blood to atone for all sin. This inaugurates a new spiritual covenant to justify all people by faith in Jesus (Matthew 26:28; 1 Corinthians 11:25; Romans 3:21-26).

The story of God finds its perfection in Jesus. God's paramount covenant is life in Christ. The old covenant is a sketch or a shadow of this Messianic covenant (Hebrews 8:5). The preacher from Hebrews compares God's previous covenants as shadows of a more perfect covenant. Does God create flawed covenants? No, the fault of the covenant lies with humanity (Hebrews 8:8-10). Humans fail to keep covenant with God, yet God remains eternally faithful. Over and over God is faithful in the face of human unfaithfulness (Jeremiah 31:31-34). The new covenant grants forgiveness. God's law is placed within our hearts. We become the people of God—the God who comes to us.

Humans now live in confidence because of Jesus' life (Hebrews 10:19-25). The call is to live forgiven lives in Christ. We hold tightly to the confession of hope. We encourage others to live in love and practice good deeds. We encourage one another. In a world after the sacrifice of Jesus, the story of God is lived differently. There is a new approach to sacrifice. In Hebrews 13:15-16, there are two ways of understanding sacrifice. Christians offer the sacrifice of praise and worship by confessing Jesus as Christ and by practicing good works and generosity.

These stories of Jesus' closest apostles and his brothers teach us about life with Jesus by the power of the spirit or the daily practice of hanging out with Jesus. The stories of Jesus' associates provide guidance for our living. When we hang around Jesus like the apostles, Jesus calls us brothers and friends. When we hang around Jesus like his own brothers, we may identify ourselves as slaves of Jesus. As Jesus' disciples our stories share these elements: live in love, be set apart for holiness, be faithful, be focused on grace, and live the promised life of Jesus. This way of discipleship—an ever changing experience of God's story—is available to everyone through the Spirit of God.

DAY 2

▷▶ DISCUSS

Small Group Discussion (60 minutes)

MOVE 1: SHARING PRAYER CONVERSATION (15 MINUTES)

- For what are you *thankful*?
- How have you *seen God at work*?
- For what are you *sorry*?
- To whom do you *need to show love*?

Move 2: *Listening to Others' Stories* (30 minutes)

- Share what you learned about yourself this week by monitoring your anger.
- In whose life story do you play a key role? Who are the people in your life story that inspire and challenge you (co-worker, family member, author, public figure, etc.)?
- With whom in your life do you discuss spiritual things?

> **Leader:** Feel free to create your own *Listening* questions.

Move 3: *Telling* Stories (10 minutes)

- The Listening Leader relates connections between the stories told by the group and the story of God from the reading or Scripture.
- For example, connect the stories shared about spiritual friendships with those people who spent time hanging around Jesus.

> **Leader:** Invite someone to share the connections they notice between God's story and our stories. By this point some have ears to hear God's activity.

Move 4: *Connecting* Conversation Prayer (5 minutes)

- This prayer time begins by reciting 1 Kings 8:23 together:

*O Lord, God of Israel, there is no God like you
in heaven above or on earth beneath,
keeping covenant and steadfast love
for your servants who walk before you with all their heart.*

- Leader ends with a prayer that reflects some of the stories and conversations from the group discussion.

> **Leader:** Before the group dismisses, describe the Echoes of God activity. Challenge group members to practice it this week.

Days 3—7

▷▷▶ PRACTICE

Echoes of God Activity

This week make a list of gadgets or technology invented in your lifetime. Keep the list with you—in a pocket or purse or on your computer or desk—and add to it throughout the week. Reflect on how each of these gadgets has (or has not) helped you become a better person.

▷▷▷▶ REFLECT

The Story & My Story

These Scripture readings and questions are for daily reflection. The first question reflects on the text and the second on "My Story." If you have less time read only the underlined chapter.

Day 3: Heb 1-7

- How has God revealed his power in this passage?
- How has God revealed his power in my life?

Day 4: Heb 8-13

- What is special about a God who makes and keeps promises?
- What are my favorite promises from God?

> **REMINDER:** Make a list of the gadgets and technology invented in your lifetime. How have these gadgets made you a better person?

Day 5: James 1-5

- What is God's role in wisdom and in temptation?
- What temptations are especially strong in my life right now?

Day 6: 1 Peter 1-5

- What is holiness in this passage?
- In what areas of my life will I allow God to make me holy?

Day 7: 1 John 1, 2, <u>3</u>–5

- How does God's love for me affect my love for others?
- Make a prayer list of the people who are the hardest for me to love.

11

Week Eleven: God Makes Everything New

This session completes the overview of the story of God from the Bible by looking at the frightening "Revelation of John." This *Reading* provides a unique overview to the Bible's most misunderstood work. The *Discussion* and *Reflection* may give you reason to see your story inside this peculiar old story. The *Practice* section challenges you to see the unseen.

Day 1

▶ READ

Stories end. The plot moves to a finale. Stories reveal conflict, tragedy, or comedy and nudge readers forward toward some resolution, misfortune, or laughter. Definitely the scariest of the stories, the Bible's last story unfortunately is the sixty-sixth and final book. Revelation mentions the mark of the beast 6-6-6 (Rev. 13:18), along with a zoo of abnormal animals that are Dr. Seuss meets Steven King. What may be done with this ending? Lots of creative things are done with Revelation in Christian books and by television preachers. The emotions summoned by Revelation are fear, confusion, uncertainty, or apathy. This ending brings endless questions. Does it predict the world's end? Are these literal events? What does the symbolism mean? Who is it about? Endings matter.

During our first year of marriage, my wife and I did not watch much television. This was good, because our ten-inch television had emotional problems. It would suddenly lose its picture. The sound remained audible but with no picture. Eventually and unpredictably the picture returned—in five minutes or three hours. Our third-hand VCR was also of questionable stability. However, one weekend we rented the movie *The Color Purple*. Halfway through the movie the tape jammed. The VCR died. Taking the VCR apart, I rescued the tape from destruction and my wallet from fees. We returned the tape without watching the end. To this day we never have seen the end of *The Color Purple*. We talk about renting and finishing it, but we never have. It has not been important. Many people treat Revelation in the same way. It is an unfinished horror movie at the Bible's end that only a scholar or a preacher can explain anyway. So, why bother?

Revelation is a beast of a book. We may prefer a different end to the Bible or even simply to understand the ending we have. When stories end with uncertainty or in unresolved ways, we are driven mad or left baffled. This chapter tells the story of Revelation in three acts, closing with three things Revelation "reveals" about life. Revelation can communicate a relevant gospel message for those who struggle with gossip, kids drugged by the pleasure of entertainment, or a sports-crazed world.

The wild story of the Revelation, or apocalypse, is given to the apostle John about Jesus Christ. Revelation literally means "revealing," but what does this story about monsters and crazy scenes reveal? Literature like Revelation discloses or brings light to some mystery. In the case of John's revelation most people feel confused. Typically the stories of apocalyptic literature surface when righteous people are in the minority and in conflict with a wicked majority. Usually these stories are told when righteous people are pessimistic about their present situation. A crisis like persecution, failure, discouragement, or death causes people to look at how things should end. While pessimistic about the present, apocalyptic literature is optimistic for the future. God's ultimate victory in Jesus is a hopeful perspective that allows people to endure present troubles.

There are four ways Christians grasp Revelation. Some treat it as a *symbolic* message for those early centuries of the church. Others see it as a *metaphor* of the evil and good in all ages. Others claim it is *history*, charting time from the Holy Spirit's arrival to the second coming of Jesus. Still others believe it is a futuristic description of the last days of a *great tribulation*. We will interpret Revelation as metaphor story for all times. Evil seems powerful at times, but God's victory is assured in Jesus Christ. When understood as a metaphor, Revelation means something to Christians in any century.

Before telling the story of Revelation, some ask about millennialism. Revelation chapter 20 mentions a thousand-year reign of Christ, or millennium, about which people spend a great deal of time thinking and worrying. Pre-millennial Christians expect Jesus to return before a thousand-year reign. They believe life will continue to get worse and evil will increase until Christ comes. Post-millennial Christians expect Jesus to come after his thousand-year reign. "Posts" believe in the power of Christian effort to Christianize the world and put emphasis on their ability to do so. A-millennialists do not interpret this as a literal earthly time period, but a metaphor that describes Christ's current reign. "A" means "non-" and designates that the church will alternate between success and persecution. My reason for treating Revelation as a metaphor (and for understanding the millennium as metaphor) comes from the words of Jesus. In Mark 13, Jesus talks about the world's end. The apostles eagerly wish to know "when" and want predictive "signs" to identify the end. Jesus explains that no one but God knows about the end—not angels and not even himself (Mark 13:32–33). If Jesus does not know, then we need not to waste time trying to know or predict when the end is to come.

The biblical story ends with Revelation, which is a story about worship. Rarely is "worship" considered an interpretive lens for this book, but the setting of the entire book is worship. Revelation has three scenes, which form a simple three-point outline. First, the Revelation is a visual message given to John while he is in worship (chapter 1). It is the Lord's Day, and John is worshiping God (1:10). John is full of the spirit and caught up in worshiping God, when he hears behind him a voice like a trumpet. The voice instructs him to write down this revelation and send it to seven churches. John turns to see who is bellowing out these instructions and through brilliant light he sees Jesus, clothed in white with a gold sash and eyes like fire. John falls down like a dead man at Jesus' feet (1:17). This is a typical response to God . . . absolute fear. Jesus reassures John not to be afraid because he is first, last, and has been alive forever. So, get busy writing, John. At two other times, John falls down in fear before heavenly beings. They tell John to get up and not worship them because they are just angels (or messengers) of God (19:1–10; 22:6–9). The book ends with John being told to "worship God" (22:9). This vision begins worshiping Jesus and ends worshiping God. The God worshiped is described in 1:4–5, "Grace to you and peace from him who is and who was and who is to come." This God has been around as past, present, and future.

The second of three scenes is a message to the seven churches in chapters 2 and 3. The message to the seven churches is about suffering and conquering. When people talk about the end of the world, they are either excited or fearful based upon what "side" they have taken. Christians may speak "triumphantly" about the end and others more fearfully. One might expect this scary story to first strike fear in the hearts of nonbelievers. Picture the bullhorn evangelist on the street corner with a sign reading, "The end of the world is near," or shouting at passersby, "Turn or burn!" to demand repentance. However, the churches repent first in this vision—not outsiders. Those in churches on the inside of God's mission are the ones God prompts to repent. The messages have a two-part refrain for each lecture. The refrains begin like this: "I know" and "to the one who conquers." Each of these seven micro-sermons express the good done but emphasize the need for change. If you conquer, then you will receive something. Like the cross, suffering is the path to victory.

To the Ephesian church, John writes these words: "I know you are doing some good things and you are hanging in there, but your first love has been abandoned" (2:2, 4). If they will return to their first love and become conquerors then they will live forever eating from the tree of life (2:7). About how many churches or Christians can it be said that they do good works and are resolved in faith, but they no longer love Jesus? Plenty fit this description.

To the church at Smyrna he writes: "I know your affliction and poverty" but do not give up (2:9). If you endure you will not be harmed (2:11b). There are churches and Christians weighed down with difficulty and ready to give up. The Laodicean church is last: I know your works, but you are lukewarm (3:15). Seven churches known by Jesus are commended and challenged. Jesus' message admits there is present suffering for Christians but challenges them to join with his conquering spirit and receive future blessings and victories. The cross of Christ gives purpose to our suffering in this life.

Our first response to suffering or evil today is not always worship. Usually, we prescribe medication, donate money, or cry tears of sorrow. We do not go worship God. When we see evil winning a victory, our first response may complain for justice, issue a lawsuit, or lament the evil in the world. Worship is rarely our first response. Worship becomes a series of components rather than regular response to God, admitting weakness without God. Revelation incites worshipful trust in Jesus, the one who conquers.

The longest scene is the third (chapters 4–22); it is a message for the church at large to worship God as evil rises. The church knows the ultimate victory of Jesus. This "message" is a spiritual vision of worship where the door to heaven is cracked open (4:1-2). John sees what will happen and it begins with ceaseless worship of God: "Holy, Holy, Holy, the Lord God the Almighty," who is God past, present, and future (4:18).

The message is that evil will continue to rise in the world (chapters 4–18). The story line is about seven seals on a scroll that cannot be opened. A lamb is found worthy to open the scroll. This lamb's (Christ's) blood opens the scroll. The story continues with seven trumpets, signs, and bowls, but it culminates with Christ as conqueror over Satan. Evil is and will be defeated. However, Christians still continue to struggle with persecution. Often, things seem lost. When the tragedy of abuse hits a family, when sexual scandal includes a minister, or when a church is closed due to division, life feels hopelessly lost. The rise of evil makes "the Revelation" a timeless story. This story of evil's strength can be written again in each generation, because evil seems to win.

However, the curtain does not fall with evil winning, because triumph is assured by Jesus' victorious conclusion (chapters 19–22). The King of Kings is source for eternal triumph. The promise of the new heaven and new earth is sealed by the God who says, "See, I am making all things new" (Revelation 21:5-6). Jesus is "coming soon" to ensure all thing are complete (Rev. 22:7, 12, 17, 20).

The Revelation of John reveals three useful things about worship. First, there is more to life than meets the eye. We live in a world that may be seen, but what moves us is *unseen* or spiritual. We invest too much energy in stories valuable only in this life. Retirement plans, landscaping, gas mileage, fashionable shoes, and new hairstyles are about rearranging the impermanent things of life. Many decisions are made using only a visual perspective rather than the eternal perspective of the Spirit. The life offered by God's Spirit invites us to live in the spiritual world of God's kingdom now.

In worship we are reminded of the hidden dimension of God's bigger perspective and activity. I cannot underestimate the value of regular public worship. Each week believers refocus on the unseen dimensions of life. We are reminded to see life with eternal eyes. We live within the larger story of God's will. At times Christians are guilty of living from a false story that failure, disappointment, and suffering are permanent.

At times our decisions or emotions are dictated by our present, visible experience. Remember that worship is our response to an unseen God. Worship puts the proper prescription on our eyes to focus through the invisible God.

Second, God is sovereign over all powers. The object of our worship is God. The eternal, almighty power of the universe is God. Life is a struggle between forces of good and forces of evil. We sometimes see a battle between Satan and God. The enemy Satan works to displace God's authority in many ways. We are seduced to trust the powers of this world, whether Roman Imperialism, American Imperialism, successful businesses, programs of education, heroes of competitive sports, or powers that demand our loyalty. God's sovereignty may not be overlooked. Each generation must answer the question of Christ versus Caesar. Will we live within the story of God's control or under Caesar's control?

Instead of giving God authority we live the false story that we are in charge. We are rulers, masters of our domain. Somehow even churches, preachers, and leaders are fooled that they call the shots to get things done. When this happens, God is not worshiped. Human wisdom, plans, and perspectives are overestimated.

Worship gives opportunity to focus upon God and break free from self-absorption. When we come to worship, we let go of a "getting things done" mentality. Christians spend time doing seemingly unproductive things like singing, praying, fasting, or reading Scripture. Yet time spent in worship shows our trust that God is sovereign.

Third, worship reminds us that Christ has conquered. The victory has been achieved for us. While there appears to be an ongoing battle against Satan—a battle God often seems to be losing—the result is assured. The final outcome already has been determined as God's victory! To be with God is to be with the winner. Evil ultimately will not win. We fear no failure. This is not about personal success, control, or victory but God's accomplishment, sovereignty, and conquest. We join God.

Sometimes Christians live in the false story that God is losing. We believe we must achieve victory for God. We blame the slackers who slow us down and credit the achievers who get things done. However, Christ has conquered already! God wins the victory. Our circumstances may bring elation with success or discouragement by failure, but we remember circumstance does not affect Christ's ultimate victory. *We endure in worship, because God will be victorious.*

One may follow the call of God on paper yet never act. We march in imaginary battles yet never leave the house. We pretend God is our commander, yet only listen for God one hour per week. This story is a vision of life lived and not of life imagined. This kingdom is real. It will be as real as it is lived. People suffer through persecution and need encouragement to go on. Life may be lived like a paperback fiction from our own pen or as a hardback volume of a real life story of faith in God. We will not live the story on paper. The ending is sure but in faith we take God's sovereign hand, trust his power for victory, and march to death and eternal life. Worship lives in God's reality.

Revelation narrates worship. We worship to remember the unseen power of the Spirit of God at work. We worship the God who is sovereign over every power. We worship to remember that Christ has won ultimate victory for God. Our primary duty is to worship and glorify God in all we say and do and believe. God on the throne says, "Behold I make all things new . . . It is done! I am the Alpha and the Omega the beginning and the end" (Rev 21:5–6). Believe the end of God's story. Believe that God has done it. No longer live in fear of suffering, but see it as preparation for the victory. The cross is the victory. Since we know how this story ends, we live the ending now. One prayer summarizes all Christian prayer from Revelation 22:20: "Come, Lord Jesus."

DAY 2

▷▶ DISCUSS

Small Group Discussion (60 minutes)

Move 1: *Sharing* Prayer Conversation (15 minutes)
- For what are you *thankful*?
- How have you *seen God at work*?
- For what are you *sorry*?
- To whom do you *need to show love*?

Move 2: *Listening* to Others' Stories (30 minutes)

- Share your reflections about technology from last week's Echoes experiment—how technology has (or has not) made you a better person.
- Tell about a time when you felt there was more to life than met the eye.
- Describe the barriers to worship in your life right now.

> **LEADER:**
> Craft your own *Listening* question to fit the unique needs of your group.

Move 3: *Telling* Stories (10 minutes)

- The Listening Leader articulates connections between the stories told in the session and the story of God from the reading or Scripture.
- For example, restate that God makes everything new. God's children focus on God's victory and join together in worshipping God. The stories we shared will find their perfection in God's time.

> **LEADER:**
> Encourage group members to make connections between God's story and our stories.

Move 4: *Connecting* Conversation Prayer (5 minutes)

- This prayer time begins by reciting 1 Kings 8:23 together:

    *O Lord, God of Israel, there is no God like you
    in heaven above or on earth beneath,
    keeping covenant and steadfast love
    for your servants who walk before you with all their heart.*

- Leader ends with a prayer that mentions some of the stories and conversations from the evening's discussion.

> **LEADER:**
> Next week is the final group meeting. Alert participants that the format will be different. There is a journaling exercise to complete before next week's group discussion. Also, describe the final Echoes activity.

Days 3—7

▷▷▶ PRACTICE

Echoes of God Activity

Observe life's unseen forces like electricity, radio waves, wireless Internet, or the power of a mother over a child. Try to think of any unseen force at work in the world. You may wish to keep a complete list to share with the group.

▷▷▷▶ REFLECT

The Story & My Story

These Scripture readings and questions are for reflection. Question one reflects on the text and the second on "My Story." If you have less time read only the underlined chapter.

Day 3: Revelation <u>1</u>-3

- What does this passage teach about God?
- When is God especially evident in my life?

Day 4: Revelation <u>4</u>-6

- Describe the worship pictured in this heavenly scene.
- How could this heavenly worship change my worship?

> **REMINDER:**
> Each day remember to practice the Echoes activity of watching for unseen forces in life.

Day 5: Revelation <u>7</u>-8

- What is the duty of creatures in heaven?
- What is my duty on earth?

Day 6: Revelation 17-<u>19</u>

- What one thing is clear to me about worship in heaven?
- What has changed about my worship of God in the last year?

Day 7: Revelation 20–22

- What is challenging about this book called Revelation?
- How did God change me by this study of the Bible?

> **REMINDER:**
> This final week has a change! There is a journaling exercise for Week Twelve that occurs before the small group meets.

12

Week Twelve: The Whole Story of God in One Story

This final week culminates with only one story as a summary of the good news of God. While many biblical stories could provide such a summary, this one story will stir the group to consider their own summary stories. We have seen how our very lives may provide context for God's activity when we listen closely for God. Complete the *Read* and *Reflect* sections before your small group *Discussion*.

DAY 1

▶ READ

"Once upon a time" is a charming way to begin a story and a peculiar way to end this story. Countless words are penned about this four-word refrain. I do not want my life story to begin "once upon a time," because it sounds like a fairy tale. My story, like your story, begins at one point in time. Today many of us live as if all stories begin "Once upon a time there was me;" we all act selfishly at some level. This final chapter narrates the whole of God's story through one story. Before telling the story, here are five principles to identify God's story.

One: Every good story begins with someone else. This someone else is outside our own experience and is a person or creature we may or may not know. A good story tells me about someone other than me, yet quickly I see myself inside the story.

Our story begins like this: "Once beyond time there was God," not you but God. This unimaginable someone only can be spoken of in terms of a hovering spirit. An eternal timeless being is present, separating the brilliance of light and the darkness of night, air and water, land and sea. God is a character beyond us.

Most readers of this guidebook may assume there is a God, but some do not assume God as a character. There are always a few thinking people who entertain the thought that humans invented God. Maybe God is something we need, like a need for a father figure. I believe we long for something that transcends this world. If one assumes there is a transcendent God, then he must be horrible. Look at God's kids. Humans horribly mistreat one another. We are prone to evil; people suffer and die. Even those who call God "Daddy" do not get the answers they want. Simply looking at God's kids shows God either is horrible or horribly absent, a dead-beat dad or a dead dad.

Let's imagine a world bigger than you. Imagine a world where you are not the center, where everything does not depend upon you. Imagine a world where you did not create yourself and that life is a story already in progress. Actually, this sounds like our experience. We do not choose to begin our lives. An amazing thing built into life is we all have a beginning. We do not pre-exist ourselves. We are dependent upon others in every way.

For example, you may or may not know your father or mother, but you have them (one of each, in fact). You may have been adopted, rejected, loved, disowned, orphaned, or thoroughbred, but you still have one father and one mother. Isn't that interesting? Your very existence depends upon other people. You had no choice whatsoever in the matter of your story's beginning. Your parents chose to create. In today's world, you may be the result of natural naked sex or the careful test-tube work of a doctor. Your beginning may have resulted from a one-night stand, a long-term marriage, or adoption papers. You had no say in the matter. Your early childhood may have been stable or stormy, forgettable or upsetting. The bottom line is you did not create yourself, but you are here in the middle of an ongoing story. You have a unique story.

Life points to something prior to itself. Life is dependent, pointing backward to conspiring creators. Similarly, it is possible to imagine God behind the bang, as a cause of the collision, as instigator of pregnancy. Just as it is obvious that you have parents; it is not a stretch to imagine something before us, someone that transcends us—like God.

Two: life is made of stories. God has written this larger story on the pages of human lives. Each person has a story of pain or joy, triumph or failure. That is life. Contemporary people are interested in stories. Some live out everyone else's story but their own. Movies, television, video games, chat rooms, instant messaging, and novels all allow vicarious living through other people's stories. Sadly our story is muted and we raise the volume on other's fictional stories. However, over these weeks we listened to other people's real stories. We told our stories. Together we have experienced a larger story includes us all.

In today's postmodern world, people cannot imagine being written into one single story. They do not like the thought of being destined to do things that are predetermined. Why would God destine people for suffering, pain, death, or disease? One single story is refused priority over other stories. "I have my story and you have yours, but do not try to force your perspective on me," we think. The postmodern world rejects this idea of a universal narrative for all people. A narrative is "a story of events or experiences whether true or fictitious." Narrative, story, and tale are synonyms used to define one another. We have seen that exploring God's story does not trump your own story. God allows you to live your own story.

Three: the Bible tells the story of God, with God as the leading character. Originally, the Bible is not one single-bound book. It is a library of books written over thousands of years about the human experience of God. The Old Testament or first testament is the story of God's activity among the Hebrew people over thousands of years. The New Testament or second testament is a story of God's activity through Jesus Christ and his earliest followers, covering fifty to one hundred years.

The Bible is a collection of books that together create a master narrative about following God. The leading role of the story is played by God. There are human experiences found on the Bible's pages, but this is the story about God. Humans were involved in writing down experiences of God, but the major character is God. Their stories and our stories are woven into a unity within the larger story of God. We may choose to allow God the lead role in our story.

Insisting upon God as primary may seem obvious, but many try to make heroes of the characters in the Bible. Abraham or Moses, Deborah or Samson, Peter or Priscilla, Paul or Ruth are exalted. However, these men and women are people like us. They screw up. They lived in different times and places and are separated by thousands of years of human history, experience, and discovery. They are not the central characters. God is the subject. From Genesis' opening line, "In the beginning, God created" to the closing book where God promises "to make all things new," this is God's story. We are invited to live our stories in participation with God.

Four: this story of God is "good news." The word "gospel" and "good news" are the same word. The gospel is God's good news. Again, I insist—unless the gospel is good news for everyone then it is not good news. While a Christian's actions and words are not always good news, the gospel of God cannot be bad news. When the gospel is presented as bad news for someone who had better change, then the gospel is no longer good.

Many times Christians tell the "good news," and it sounds horrible. The good news lists propositions on which believers must affirm. The good news is crammed with creeds to be memorized. Gospel is reduced to church tradition. However, these are not at the center of good news nor do they sound like good news to a world desperate for good news. Worst of all, many Christians describe the good news in terms of who is in "God's grace," as if God's grace were an exclusive club. We tragically miss the mark of good news. The good news is great news for everyone in every place in every time. The good news is our shared story. The only bad news is the sad news of those who choose to dismiss good news. This rejection is sad news, but it is not the gospel! John 3:16-17 expresses that God loves all people and he chose to die for and to save the whole world. Even if we think it is another scam offer, God sent Jesus to save and not condemn the world. God's news is good.

Five: you are invited into this story of God. For most of you, this book is the first time you have heard the story from the beginning of Genesis all the way to your story. This book does not claim that you now "know the story" but is an experience of connecting your story and God's story. It may be surprising to discover that the story of God is not merely something that happened a long time ago in a remote corner of the world, but it happens with every sunrise of your life. Your story is the one you know best. You may have been surprised to see God in your story. God has been there all along. God wants to take a more active part in your life than ever before. This book is an invitation to be holy like God. Jesus invites us to follow him. The Holy Spirit is our invitation to live like God today. And now I present the whole story of God and his desire for relationship with you through one story that Jesus spoke long ago. May the eternal God, by his living Word, breathe his Holy Spirit into you today.

A Story

Once there was a dad with two sons. The older son is smart and responsible and available. The younger son is not much of anything. One day the younger son says, "Dad I wish you were already dead. I know I have an inheritance coming and I would like to have it now." The son does not want his father. He wants something *from* his father. For good or bad, the dad divides his possessions and property in half and gives the younger son his inheritance early. The smiling young son converts it all to cash within days and leaves for an exciting new place. The young man eats, drinks, smokes, snorts, shoots, experiences, and sleeps with everything and everyone. Men and women are available to him until his tank is drained completely.

Unfortunately, the economy crashes simultaneously with the collapse of the young man's cash. There is no work available except the job of cleaning the public restrooms and dumpsters of this foreign city. He is a homeless foreigner with a past and no future. Life at the bottom smells painfully rancid to his once pampered nose, now stuck in filth.

The drug of pleasure wears off and he comes to his senses. Things do not have to be this way. He is worse off than the least of his dad's employees. Even though he is now worthless, he could do this same menial job in his home country. He could go to his father, own his destructive life, and request to clean the bathrooms and dumpsters at his own home. He goes home practicing his begging speech.

Little does he know that his father anticipates his return. With a crowd of frowning faces and shaking heads behind him, the father spots the filthy son from a distance and runs wildly to his son. He hugs his filthy son and kisses his cracked, dry lips. "Dad, I messed up. I sinned against God. I sinned against you. I do not deserve to be your son."

Before the son can ask for a job, the father strips off his own clean clothes and jewelry as a sign that the dad's clothes are his son's clothes. The son is bathed, cleaned, probably bathed again, scrubbed, and clothed in his father's finest clothing. There are no conditions or probations or lectures given by the father. The father welcomes the son home.

The father throws a citywide party for his now more "experienced" son. The reason given is that his son was dead but now is alive again. This son, who was on the missing person milk carton, now is in the newspaper. They party! Even though the town thinks this father is crazy to welcome home a juvenile delinquent, they celebrate just the same.

Everyone celebrates except one person. The older responsible son, the real heir was out in the field finishing a full day's work. He hears the music, smells the food, sees the crowds, and asks what is going on. This party is for his good-for-nothing brother. He hears the detailed description and feels his jaw tighten. He refuses to go inside for the celebration. He fights with his father, disrespectfully demanding, "Listen! Love me more because I am the faithful son." The dad lovingly affirms the oldest son is loved and still has his full inheritance. He needs to celebrate the resurrection of his lost brother. A juvenile delinquent who was dead is now alive; he was lost and now is found.

Jesus tells this story because religious people questioned Jesus' practice of hanging out with financial swindlers and whores (Luke 15:1-2). Jesus tells the story to show us God's love and our identity. This is the whole story—our story. Trouble happens when we write our story with us as the hero. When we attempt to live our life alone, God is not at the center of the story. This story celebrates those who live in the kingdom of the Father. This is the story of Israel, it is the story of America, and it is my story. The entire world is God's family. Some children leave, some stay, but all are children of God.

The whole story is told in four moves. First is the setting—God gives life. God is creator and father. Second, the conflict comes as God lets us go. This God permits us to act like children. He lets us fail miserably. Third, the climax is God's constant love. Even while we are gone, God anticipates our return. Third, the resolution is God's celebration of our return. God schedules no repayment plan. God unconditionally welcomes us home. In Zephaniah 3:17, there is a tear-jerking image of God. God is a warrior who wins victory for us, and then he sings over us. God sings his heart out over our forgiveness, our pain, and our difficulties.

At this moment in the story, which child are you: rebellious or faithful? At what point are you in the story today: trash heap, pouting outside, or celebrating inside? There is one God, who is the hero. We exist at God's pleasure in this story. We may live at our discretion inside or outside the house, in a foreign dumpster or in the clothes of God. You are invited into a much larger story. God is at work in this world, bringing a new world. God creates us. God loves us. God lets us go. God celebrates when we embrace our identity as children of God.

Week Twelve: The Whole Story of God in One Story

▷▶ REFLECT

Journal Exercise Reflecting on The Story & My Story

In order to assess our progress through the story of God, spend time journaling answers to these questions *before* the small group meeting. Bring this pre-work journal to the last small group discussion.

1. How would you summarize the story of the Bible to a friend in a short conversation?
2. Imagine someone asked you to summarize "the gospel" in a few words. What would you tell them (See chapter 7. Use experience, story, song, movie, etc.)?
3. In what specific ways have you experienced the story of God connecting with routine activities of your life?
4. Relate some of your memorable experiences of listening and echoing through this process.
5. Write about how your practice of prayer developed during this time.

> **LEADER:**
>
> The assessment exercise is an informal survey that is completed in a conversational style. Bring a notepad and write some notes about people's comments. Their answers to these questions will give you a good idea of the changes they have experienced over the twelve weeks.

Day 2

> **LEADER:**
>
> This week is slightly different. This discussion time reflects and examines the entire experience of the program. Help the group use the now familiar discussion structure to briefly and prayerfully review the entire experience.

▷▷▶ DISCUSS

Final Small Group Conversation: Assessment Exercise

As the group draws to a close with this session, notice that the four moves have been altered. Prior to the small group meeting complete both the *Read* section and journal through the *Reflect* sections above. The Sharing move examines the entire twelve-week group experience. The Listening and

Telling moves are combined into a longer discussion as an Assessment Exercise. The purpose of this last gathering is to bring things to a close and reflect on the group's journey together.

Move 1: *Sharing* Prayer Conversation (15 minutes)

- For what are you *thankful* about this experience?
- How have you *seen God at work* in this group experience?
- For what are you *sorry* or regret about this time?
- To whom does our group *need to show love*?

Moves 2 & 3: *Listening* & *Telling* Assessment Exercise (40 minutes)

1. What have you learned about God or the Bible in this process? (Cognitive)
2. What new things have you come to believe (about God, self, or life) because of this experience? (Affective)
3. Describe any new habits or actions you have developed through these weeks. (Behavior)
4. Share any new skills you have learned or experienced or improved. (Skill)

Move 4: *Connecting* Conversation Prayer (5 minutes)

- This prayer time begins by reciting 1 Kings 8:23 together:

> *O Lord, God of Israel, there is no God like you in heaven above or on earth beneath, keeping covenant and steadfast love for your servants who walk before you with all their heart.*

- Leader ends with a prayer that celebrates the conversations and experiences from the entire three months. The Leaders' notes made during the evening provide a ready reference for connections that may be made in this prayer. Specifically thank God for how the story of God has visibly continued today through our lives as a result of this time.

What's next?

Before the group concludes, talk about how this approach could be used next. What do the group participants and leaders intend to do next with what they have experienced?

Day 3

▷▷▷▶ PRACTICE

Good for you—you made it through a long story in a short time period! I pray you enjoyed this narrative journey and found yourself inside of a much more significant story. While this experience is ending, it is now up to you to begin using this on your own. You may choose to use this approach with a new group or you might continue as a group using the small group format to continue meeting. You may choose to start a lunch listening group, a movie-watching club, or a discussion group in an apartment complex. Some may choose to use the very simple four-move discussion format with a group of people who are unfamiliar with the way of Jesus. Use this week to reflect and prayerfully ask God to help you identify how and where you can listen to others in a weekly setting and in everyday informal conversation.

> *What will I do next?*
>
> Ask God to send you another person with whom you could share this process. Prayerfully consider what elements of this process should remain spiritual disciplines in your life.

Bibliography

Fee, Gordon D., and Douglas Stuart. *How to Read the Bible for all it is Worth*. 2nd ed. Grand Rapids, MI: Zondervan, 1993.

Job, Rueben P., and Norman Shawchuck. *A Guide to Prayer*. Nashville: The Upper Room, 1983.

Newbigin, Lesslie. *A Walk through the Bible*. Louisville, KY: Westminster John Knox, 1999.

Nouwen, Henri J. M. *In the Name of the Father: Reflections on Christian Leadership*. New York: Crossroads, 1999.

Redmount, Carol A. "Bitter Lives: Israel in and out of Egypt." In *The Oxford History of the Biblical World*, edited by Michael D. Coogan, 79–121. New York: Oxford University Press: 1999.

Willard, Dallas. *Hearing God: Developing a Conversational Relationship with God*. Downers Grove, IL: InterVarsity (1999).

www.ingramcontent.com/pod-product-compliance
Lightning Source LLC
Chambersburg PA
CBHW050832160426
43192CB00010B/1997